Daily Devotions for Die-Hard Kids

TO PARENTS/GUARDIANS FROM THE AUTHOR

DAILY DEVOTIONS FOR DIE-HARD KIDS is an adaptation of our DAILY DEVOTIONS FOR DIE-HARD FANS series. It is suggested for children ages 6 to 12, but that guideline is, of course, flexible. Only the parents or other adults can appraise the spiritual maturity of their children.

The devotions are written with the idea that a parent or adult will join the children to act as a mentor and spiritual guide for each devotion and the discussion that may ensue. The devotions seek to engage the child by capitalizing on his or her interest in the particular collegiate team the family follows. The interest in college sports is thus an oblique and somewhat tricky way, if you will, to lead your children to reading the Bible and learning about God, Jesus, and faith.

Each devotion contains a short Bible reading (except for occasional longer stories that must be read in their entirety), a paraphrase of the most pertinent scripture verse, a true LSU sports story, and a theological discussion that ties everything together through a common theme. The devotion then concludes with a suggested activity that is based on the theme of the day. I tie each day's theological message to a child's life by referring to such aspects as school, household chores, video games, and relations with parents, siblings, and teachers, etc.

The devotions are intended to be fun for both the adult and the child, but they are also intended to be attempts to spark interest in quite serious matters of faith and living a godly life. A point of emphasis throughout the book is to impress upon the child that faith is not just for the times when the family gathers for formal worship in a particular structure, but rather is for every moment of every day wherever he or she may be.

Our children are under attack by the secular world as never before. It is a time fraught with danger for the innocence and the faith of our most precious family members. I pray that this book will provide your children with a better understanding of what it means to be a Christian. I also pray that this book will help lay the foundation for what will be a lifelong journey of faith for your children. May God bless you and your family.

ED MCMINN

Daily Devotions for Die-Hard Kids: LSU TIGERS

© 2016 Ed McMinn; Extra Point Publishers; P.O. Box 871; Perry GA 31069

To order books or for more information, visit us at die-hardfans.com
Cover design by John Powell and Slynn McMinn;
Interior design by Slynn McMinn

DAILY DEVOTIONS FOR DIE-HARD FANS

ACC
CLEMSON TIGERS
DUKE BLUE DEVILS
FSU SEMINOLES
GA. TECH YELLOW JACKETS
NORTH CAROLINA TAR HEELS
NC STATE WOLFPACK
NOTRE DAME FIGHTING IRISH
VIRGINIA CAVALIERS
VIRGINIA TECH HOKIES

BIG 12
BAYLOR BEARS
OKLAHOMA SOONERS
OKLAHOMA STATE COWBOYS
TCU HORNED FROGS
TEXAS LONGHORNS
TEXAS TECH RED RAIDERS
WEST VIRGINIA MOUNTAINEERS

BIG 10
MICHIGAN WOLVERINES
NEBRASKA CORNHUSKERS
OHIO STATE BUCKEYES
PENN STATE NITTANY LIONS

SEC
ALABAMA CRIMSON TIDE
MORE ALABAMA CRIMSON TIDE
ARKANSAS RAZORBACKS
AUBURN TIGERS
MORE AUBURN TIGERS
FLORIDA GATORS
GEORGIA BULLDOGS
MORE GEORGIA BULLDOGS
KENTUCKY WILDCATS
LSU TIGERS
MISSISSIPPI STATE BULLDOGS
MISSOURI TIGERS
OLE MISS REBELS
SOUTH CAROLINA GAMECOCKS
MORE S. CAROLINA GAMECOCKS
TEXAS A&M AGGIES
TENNESSEE VOLUNTEERS

NASCAR

DAILY DEVOTIONS FOR DIE-HARD KIDS
ALABAMA CRIMSON TIDE; BAYLOR BEARS; AUBURN TIGERS;
GEORGIA BULLDOGS; LSU TIGERS MISS. STATE BULLDOGS;
OLE MISS REBELS; TEXAS LONGHORNS; TEXAS A&M AGGIES

3

IN THE BEGINNING

Read Genesis 1:1; 2:1-3.

In the beginning, God created the heavens and the earth.

A chemistry teacher started LSU football.

His name was Charles E. Coates. He came to teach at the Louisiana Seminary of Learning and Military Academy and was surprised to find no athletics. He felt a whole man should be a scholar and an athlete.

So in the fall of 1893, he set out to change the situation. He joined forces with another professor to enlist some players. They had no uniforms; they nailed cleats on leather shoes.

Word soon got around town about the daily scrimmages, and folks got excited about this new game they had never seen. The first LSU game was on Nov. 25, 1893, against Tulane. The game was played in New Orleans.

Fans rode the train with special rates of

$1.50 per ticket. Tickets for the game were 50 cents each.

Almost 2,000 people showed up for the contest even though the weather was cold. Each team chose a ref, and Tulane won.

Football at LSU had begun.

The school then hired a paid coach. The next time they played Tulane, LSU won 8-4 in 1895.

Beginnings are important, but how we use those beginnings is even more important. You get a new beginning in your life every time the sun comes up and brings you a new day.

Have you ever thought that every morning is a gift from God? Well, it is. This present of a new day shows God's love for you. Each new day is full of promise. You can use it to make some wrong things right and to do some good.

How you use your new day is up to you. You should just make sure you walk with God all day long.

Try starting each morning by thanking God for the day and asking him to protect and lead you all day long.

DAY 2

BLUEGRASS MIRACLE

Read Matthew 12:38-40.

Jesus said, "Wicked and unfaithful people ask for miracles" to convince them he is Lord and Savior.

Kentucky students ran onto the field to celebrate a win. The Wildcat head coach had been soaked with Gatorade. The scoreboard read UK 30 LSU 27. But then came what LSU fans call The Bluegrass Miracle. (Ask an adult what bluegrass has to do with Kentucky.)

In 2002, LSU trailed Kentucky with only two seconds on the clock. The Tigers had the ball on their own 25. Wildcat fans and players were already celebrating their big win.

But then quarterback Marcus Randall threw the ball as far as he could. It came down in the middle of a whole bunch of players from both teams.

Three Kentucky players touched the ball. The

fourth player to touch the bouncing ball was LSU's Devery Henderson. He grabbed it out of the air at the UK 18, juggled it, and then ran into the end zone. LSU won 33-30.

"It was like a dream," Henderson said. "I couldn't believe it." Neither could the Wildcats and their fans. Their party was ruined by the Bluegrass Miracle.

A miracle is something that you can't explain except by saying God did it. Some people say miracles are rare, but they are wrong.

Since God made the world and everything in it, the whole world is a miracle. You are a miracle! Just think: There's nobody else in the world like you. You're so special God made only one of you (unless you're a twin!).

A lot of people don't see miracles around them because they don't have any faith in God. Jesus knew that seeing a miracle doesn't make someone believe in him. But since you believe in Jesus and God, you can see miracles.

List some things around you that are miracles because God made them.

DAY 3

ALL IN

Read Mark 12:28-31.

"Love the Lord your God with all your heart, all your soul, all your mind, and all your strength."

When Matt Flynn committed to play quarterback for LSU, he really went all in.

Flynn arrived in Baton Rouge in 2003, but JaMarcus Russell was there, too. He spent four seasons on the bench. He held for extra points and field goals and played a little when the Tigers were way ahead.

Frustrated, he thought about transferring to another school so he could play. But he had committed and he didn't want to go back on his word. So he waited for his time.

That came in 2007. A senior, Flynn quarterbacked the Tigers all the way to the national championship game. Then, against Ohio State, he threw four touchdown passes. The Tigers romped to a 38-24 win and the national title.

Flynn was named the game's offensive MVP. He had that honor and the title because of his commitment to LSU.

"It's been tough" he said about waiting so long. "But right now, it's so, so sweet."

What is it that you really like so much that you'd do it all the time if you could? It's called having "zeal" or "enthusiasm" for something. For instance, do you jump up and down and whoop and holler when the Tigers score?

What about your zeal for the Lord? On Sunday morning, if you go to church at all, do you pretty much act like you're getting your teeth cleaned or you're about to get a shot?

Jesus made it clear which rule is number one to God. You are to be all in for God, to love him with all your heart, all your soul, all your mind, all your strength.

You are to be fired up for God! Are you?

Promise God that at church Sunday you will sing real loud and will listen to the sermon and not talk all through it.

LIVE ACTION

Read James 2:14-17.

Faith without action is dead.

Auburn talked. Leonard Fournette ran. Game to LSU.

Before the 2015 game, an Auburn player bragged that it "shouldn't be too difficult" to stop Fournette, LSU's star running back. Head coach Les Miles had the comments put up in Fournette's locker so he could read them. "Everybody was pretty mad about it," Fournette said about the trash talk.

It took one play for the whole Auburn team to regret all that talk. On LSU's first snap, Fournette ripped off a 71-yard run. That was only the beginning. He spent the next three quarters "humiliating Auburn defenders." They never even slowed Fournette down; they certainly couldn't stop him.

The Tigers destroyed Auburn 45-21. Fournette rushed for 228 yards and scored three touchdowns. Auburn tried everything it could to stop Fournette, even jumping on his head. Nothing worked.

"It was fun," Fournette said after the game.

Talk is cheap. By itself, it just isn't worth too much as Auburn found out against LSU. How much fun is it to sit around and listen to somebody talk? You get all squirmy because you want to get up and do something.

It's that way in your faith life. In church, you may like singing songs and watching baptisms. But sitting through a sermon sometimes is hard, isn't it?

Even Jesus didn't just talk. He almost never was still. He constantly moved from one place to another, healing and helping people.

Just talking about your faith doesn't really show it. You show that Jesus is alive by making your faith alive. You act. You do the kinds of things for people that Jesus did.

List some things you can do tomorrow to show that your faith is alive. Do them.

RAINDROPS

Read Genesis 9:8-15.

The waters of a flood will never destroy all life again.

The 2003 football season ended with a national title. It began with a bad thunderstorm.

LSU played Louisiana-Monroe in the season opener. Each team ran a few plays and didn't do much. Then suddenly, God decided to put on a show.

Lightning popped, thunder rolled, and rain started coming down in sheets. All that bad weather forced the refs to stop play. Players, fans, and coaches hurried for cover to get out of the downpour.

The rain delay lasted 40 minutes. When the rain let up a little bit, the game started again. But the Tigers just kind of sloshed around for a while. Suddenly, though, quarterback Matt Mauck got as hot as Louisiana lightning.

Tigers

Mauck threw three touchdown passes in the second quarter. The Tigers showed they could play good football in the mud. Despite the rain delay and the wet field, they won 49-7.

Hey, rain is a good thing, isn't it? It makes the crops grow so you can eat. It keeps the grass green and pretty. It's fun to run around in, and it makes puddles to stomp in.

But rain sometimes wipes out fun things like your baseball game, a family picnic, or a swim party. Rain's not a very good thing then.

We don't have any control over the rain. It doesn't really care what you want to do; it's going to fall when and where it wants to. That's because God is in charge of the rain.

God is in charge of your life, too. One strange thing, though: He will control your life only if you let him. When you walk with God, it's like walking in the sunshine even when it's raining.

With a gauge, measure how much rain falls next time. Thank God for the rain. Keep track of the rainfall for a week.

NEW STUFF

Read Hebrews 8:6-9.

*The new covenant is better than
the old one. It has better promises.*

LSU's softball players finally made what was
called "the longest one-mile move in history."

That move came in 2009 when a brand new
Tiger Park opened. Since 2004, the softball
head coach had been telling recruits that they
would be playing in a brand new stadium.

But several setbacks — including Hurricane
Katrina — delayed construction. All-American
catcher Killian Roessner never dreamed she
wouldn't play in the new place, but she didn't.

Why was LSU so eager to throw away the
old park? It was only twelve years old, built
in 1997 when LSU softball began. The Tigers
sure could win there. Their record was 338-51.

But the head coach said the old field was
not a stadium but a park. "We have no locker

room here," she said. "For years, there were no bathrooms here. There was no place for fans to park."

So on Feb. 11, 2009, the new Tiger Park replaced the old one. It was like old times; the team won the first game there 6-0.

There's nothing quite like getting new stuff, is there? Maybe a new phone, or a new bike or video game. New things are exciting and fun!

God has given you something new in Jesus. A long time ago, God made some promises to some folks called the Israelites. This set of promises is called a covenant or agreement. But then came Jesus, and God made a new and better covenant that includes everyone, especially you.

It's a new way for you to get to Heaven and live with God and Jesus forever. What you have to do is believe in Jesus and live like it. God does the rest, keeping his new promises.

Find some stuff in your room that used to be new but is now old. Like Jesus, is the new stuff better?

UNDER PRESSURE

Read Matthew 26:36-39.

Jesus said, "My soul is sad. I feel close to death."

The 1972 football season is called the "Year of the Miracle." That's because of the Ole Miss game when quarterback Bert Jones led "the best pressure drive in Tiger Stadium history."

The Rebels led 16-10 when the Tigers got the ball at their own 20. The clock read 3:01, and LSU had only one timeout left.

Jones quickly led the team down the field to the Rebel 20. LSU used its last timeout with ten seconds on the clock. Coach Charlie McClendon huddled with his calm quarterback and called a play. Then he said, "Bert, this is what you came to LSU for." After the game the head Tiger told reporters, "You know what he did? He winked at me!"

A penalty and an incomplete pass moved

the ball to the 10-yard line with one second left. Feeling no pressure, Jones found tailback Brad Davis for a touchdown! Rusty Jackson stayed calm under pressure by booting the game-winning extra point. 17-16, LSU.

Even as a kid, you live every day with pressure. You have to make good grades. You have to do your homework. You always have projects to finish and adults to keep happy.

Pressure can drive you to do your best. Or it can make you cry with fear. But God is right there to help you with the pressures of daily living. You pray. God will give you the grace to hang on and do your best if you ask. Just as he did Jesus when he faced the pressure of the death that waited for him.

Just remember. The most pressure of all lies in deciding where you will spend eternity. And you've taken care of that by deciding to follow Jesus. The pressure's off — forever.

Pray for God to help you. Then practice being under pressure by trying to say the alphabet in under seven seconds.

BE PREPARED

Read Matthew 10:5-16.

*Go into the world and be as wise as
snakes and as innocent as doves.*

The Tigers beat top-ranked Florida in 1997
28-21. But they really won the game before
the kickoff when they prepared themselves in
the meeting room long before the kickoff.

The upset win came on two touchdowns in
the fourth quarter. The victory was no fluke.
It happened because of careful planning by
head coach Gerry DiNardo and his staff. They
came up with a game plan that quarterback
Herb Tyler and the offense pulled off perfectly.
The prepared defense did its part, too.

DiNardo decided to "smack Florida in the
mouth" on offense. So LSU just ran the ball
right up the middle time after time. It worked
as the Tigers rushed for 158 yards.

The LSU coaches kept the defensive starters

fresh by getting some of the reserves into the action all game long. This worked, too, as the Gators had only 49 yards rushing. The defense also had five sacks and four interceptions.

The prepared Tigers had their first win over a No.-1 ranked team in their history..

Anytime LSU plays any game, the coaches and the players spend time preparing so they can win. It's the same way for you, isn't it?

When you have a test at school, you prepare by studying. You prepare for a baseball game or a soccer game or a 4-H competition or a play at church by practicing for it.

Jesus prepared his followers, too. He knew he was going to die on the cross. He wanted them to be ready to spread the good news even after he went to Heaven.

You read the Bible and go to Sunday school and church. It's all to prepare you for the day you finally see Jesus face-to-face.

List the things you do in the morning to prepare for each day (like brush your teeth). Is a prayer on that list?

TRICK PLAYS

Read Acts 19:11-16.

*Some tricksters tried to use Jesus'
name to drive out evil spirits. They
wound up naked and bleeding.*

LSU once pulled off a trick play so daring a coach would be crazy to try it today.

LSU's 1935 football team went 9-1 and won the SEC championship. The showdown in the SEC came against Georgia on Nov. 16.

The game was scoreless when the Tigers used some bold trickery to score. They were backed up to their own 4-yard line. So they lined up to punt just like everyone expected. Halfback Abe Mickal went way back in the end zone to do the kicking. (Mickal was so good he is a member of the College Football Hall of Fame.)

Mickal got a good snap from the center. He stepped forward and swung his foot like he was punting. Instead, he handed the ball behind his back to halfback Jesse Fatherree. Fatherree took off down the left sideline and kept going and kept going — and kept going.

He covered 106 yards, all the way into the Georgia end zone for a touchdown. Some big-time "trickeration" had completely fooled the Bulldogs. LSU went on to win 13-0.

How funny is it that those tricksters in the Bible wound up running around whooping and hollering without any clothes on? Some tricks people play are fun, but some are not.

Some people will try to trick you by leading you away from God's word or Jesus. You have to be careful. They may try to trick you by telling you that what Jesus said isn't really true, that he isn't really the Son of God.

It's a funny thing about Jesus. His good news does sound too good to be true: Believe in him and you are saved and will go to Heaven one day. But it's true. It's no trick.

Think about a trick somebody played on you. How did it make you feel?

DAY 10

RUN FOR IT

Read John 20:1-10.

Peter and the other disciple ran to Jesus' tomb.

An LSU running back was just awful starting out. His coach had to keep telling him things would get better. And, boy, did they ever.

Charles Alexander was All-America and All-SEC in both 1977 and 1978. He was the SEC Most Valuable Player in 1977. He is a member of the LSU Athletic Hall of Fame.

In his first varsity game, though, Alexander ran the ball eight times and gained a grand total of minus two yards! After the game, head coach Charlie McClendon patted Alexander on the back and told him that "things would get better." The unhappy freshman just hung his head and didn't say anything.

Things did get better in the next game, but not by very much. Alexander ran the ball eight times again — for three yards. So far, he had carried the ball sixteen times and gained one pitiful yard. Again, the head coach had to tell him things would get better.

They did as Alexander ran to stardom and gained the nickname "Alexander the Great."

You probably do a lot of running. You run at recess and at PE. Spot a playground and you run to it without thinking. You run during a game, whether it's softball, soccer, or basketball. You run a race to see who's the fastest.

But no matter how hard, how far, or how fast you run, you can never outrun God. You can run from Baton Rouge to California, but God is right there with you every step of the way. God wants you to run — right to Jesus. Life is like a long race, and the only way to win it is by running it step by step with Jesus.

Here's something odd. The best way to run to Jesus is to drop to your knees — and pray.

If it's not dark yet, go out and run around your house, picturing Jesus running with you all the way.

GET WELL SOON

Read Matthew 17:14-18.

Jesus healed the boy at that very moment.

For two years, Jarvis Green played football in constant pain. He hurt so bad he couldn't even tie his shoes. And then he prayed.

Green was an LSU defensive end in 1998 and '99. All the while, he was in pain from a bad back. "It was killing me," he said. "I had to lay in bed to do everything, including putting my shoes on."

The pain came from a minor car wreck. He played with it, but it kept getting worse. As the 2000 season was about to begin, the pain was so bad that he probably would be able to play only part-time.

And then God stepped in. After the last pre-season scrimmage, Green prayed for about thirty minutes. When he awoke the next morning, the pain was gone. He got so excited, he flapped his arms, jumped on his bed, and hit the wall so hard he woke up his roommate.

"I was scared the pain might come up again," he said during the season. "But it never did." God had taken it away for good. Green went on to a pro career.

When you get sick or get hurt, what do you do? You tell your mom or your dad, take some medicine, and maybe go to the doctor. If it gets really bad, you wind up in the hospital. That's no fun at all.

You should be doing all that, but have you ever prayed for God to heal you? He is the one who made your body so that it heals itself like when you get a cold or a cut. He's also the one who made the doctors and nurses smart enough to help you get well.

God is the greatest healer of all. He should be a part of your getting well soon.

Recall the last time you were sick or hurt. List everything that was done. Then figure out how God was in each step.

DAY 12

MEETING SOMEONE

Read Luke 24:13-23, 31-34.

Two men were walking to a village, and Jesus joined them.

A meeting in Europe that was an accident changed LSU basketball history.

Dale Brown is LSU's winningest men's basketball coach. In 1986, he was on a tour putting on some coaching clinics in Europe. At a U.S. Army base in Germany, he showed off some trick shots for a crowd.

Watching was a teenager who thought the LSU coach was "real funny." He didn't even know who Dale Brown was, but he liked the coach's trick shots and met him after the show.

The kid stood 6-feet-6, and Brown thought he was a soldier. He asked what his rank was. "I'm 13 years old," came the answer. The next question was, "Your dad around?"

The teen was Shaquille O'Neal, one of the

greatest players in LSU and NBA history.

When Shaq's family came home to New Jersey, he found a stack of letters from Brown at his grandmother's house. "I got about 2,000 letters from Coach Brown," he said.

And from a lucky meeting, LSU got a legend.

Even as a kid, the people you meet change your life because you are always meeting new people. Sometimes you just bump into them by chance. That means you don't plan to meet someone; you kind of meet them by accident. Like on a playground or in a park. Or at a football game or in the school lunchroom.

But some meetings are too important to be left to chance. Like meeting Jesus. You have to seek him out. You go to church, you read your Bible, you pray, you talk about him with a friend or with an adult teacher. How you meet Jesus doesn't matter; what matters is that you find him.

Once you do, you have a best friend for life.

Name three friends of yours.
Then tell how you met them.

BY THE RULES

Read Luke 5:27-32.

Some religious leaders complained because Jesus broke the rules and ate with sinners.

Head coach Paul Dietzel used a change in the rules to create an LSU legend.

Dietzel coached LSU football from 1955-61 The new rules in 1958 let him substitute freely, so he divided his Tigers into three teams.

The third team was a bunch of second-team linemen and third-string backs. They would play nothing but defense. Dietzel nicknamed them the Chinese Bandits from a comic strip.

In the second game, Dietzel put them in with Alabama at the 5-yard line. "It took guts," said a coach because it meant taking the first-team defense out! Alabama ran three plays and gained one yard. LSU won 13-3, and the legend of the Chinese Bandits was born.

Tigers

They became national stars. When a magazine did a story on LSU, they focused on the Bandits. They were so good they held teams to less than one yard per play for the season!

LSU won the national title, led by a bunch of subs who played because of a rules change.

Like football players, you live with a whole set of rules. Go to bed at a certain time. Mind your parents. Don't act ugly to your brother or sister. Be polite to your teachers.

Rules are hard but they aren't always bad things. Without them, our whole world and our country would be a mess. Nobody would get along, and people couldn't do stuff together.

The rules Jesus didn't like were those that said some people should be treated badly. He broke them, and he expects you to do it, too. You should never mistreat anybody just because somebody says it's the thing to do.

Jesus loves that person. So should you.

Think of a rule that you don't like.
Why do you think you have it?
What would happen if you broke it?

WINNING

Read 1 John 5:1-6.

The person who believes Jesus is the son of God is the real winner in the world.

A newspaper once said LSU won a football game without winning.

It happened way back in 1896. Tulane led 2-0 when a player was injured. A sub ran onto the field, but LSU didn't like it. The Tigers said he was an illegal player. It seems the teams had agreed to sign papers before the game that said all the players were students. The Tulane sub hadn't signed the papers.

The referee was a military instructor at LSU. He agreed with LSU, which really upset the Tulane players. Their captain wouldn't order the illegal player out of the game. So the referee said Tulane had forfeited the game by refusing to play without him.

That brought up a big yell from some LSU fans, but most everybody was unhappy. After all, they had wanted to see a football game.

The ref set the final game of the game LSU won without winning at 6-0.

To compete means to try to beat somebody else at something. All of life is a competition; it's not just football or soccer games. You compete against others at school for a good seat in the lunchroom. You try to beat others in a video game.

Competition isn't bad for you as long as you play according to the rules the way that LSU's teams do. It makes you stronger.

In everything you do, you should want to win. Winning isn't everything, but you should always try to do your best. Sometimes you will lose, but you don't quit trying.

Only with your faith in Jesus do you never lose. You win — every time and for all time.

Name some things in which you competed and won and some you lost. Did they make you feel different? How?

DAY 15

FAMILY TIES

Read Mark 3:31-35.

Jesus said, "Whoever does God's will is my family."

Todd Kinchen was born to play football for LSU. It was what his family did.

His dad was a Chinese Bandit from 1958-60. His uncle played center for the Tigers from 1960-62. His brother was an LSU All-SEC tight end in the late 1980s.

His mother was an LSU cheerleader for four years. She was twice the homecoming queen. The school changed the rules after that so nobody could win more than once.

In 1990, Todd put his name into the family's book of LSU football lore. Against 11th-ranked Texas A&M, he had what was called one of the most spectacular two minutes in LSU history.

In the fourth quarter, Todd grabbed a short pass and turned it into a 79-yard touchdown.

Tigers

Then seconds later, he returned a punt 60 yards to set up another touchdown. His two big plays led LSU to a 17-8 upset of A&M.

Todd was just doing what the Kinchen family always did: playing football for LSU.

Somebody once said that families are like fudge, mostly sweet with a few nuts. You can probably name your sweet kinfolks — and the nutty ones too.

You may not like it all the time, but you have a family. Hey, you can blame God for that. God loves the idea of family so much that he chose to live in one as a son, a brother, and a cousin. Jesus had a family.

But Jesus also had a new definition for what makes up a family. It's not just blood. It's a choice. Everybody who does God's will is a member of Jesus' family.

That includes you. You have family members all over the place who stand ready to love you because you're all part of God's big family.

With help from a parent or grandparent, draw your family tree.

DAY 16

JOIN THE CROWD

Read Hebrews 12:1-3

A huge crowd of witnesses is all around us.

Not long ago, LSU played a football game in a Tiger Stadium that was about half full.

It happened in the first game of the 2008 season. One of the reasons for the small crowd was the kickoff time: 10 o'clock. In the morning! "It's the earliest kickoff I've ever had except when I was in the ninth grade," head coach Les Miles said.

The Tigers ate their pregame meal at 6:30 and were on the practice field at 9. "You got up, ate some grits, and were ready to roll," said linebacker Darry Beckwith. He also said, "I'm not a morning person."

Why the early start? The threat of Hurricane Gustav. It was start early or cancel the game.

So the stadium showed a lot of empty seats

for the kickoff. The small crowd or the early start didn't bother the Tigers. They jumped out to an early 31-0 lead and won easily.

The crowd then got even smaller as the home folks left the game early to find some air conditioning or some shade.

You don't have a big crowd of folks cheering for you like the Tigers do. No TV cameras follow you around. But you're almost always in a crowd. At school, at church, on the playground — there are people all around you.

There's another crowd all around you that you probably don't think about. That's all the folks who, like you, follow Jesus. Being a Christian isn't easy. All those grown-up Christians, the teen-aged Christians, and the kids your age who are Christians can help you.

Even when you're by yourself, you've never alone. You see, God is with you; God is part of the crowd standing by you, cheering for you.

Count each crowd you're in today or tomorrow. Remember to count God each time. What was the biggest one?

I KNOW THAT!

Read John 4:25-26, 39-42.

"We know that this man really is the Savior of the world."

Everyone claimed to know something, which they didn't. One LSU player did know something, which led to the SEC title.

On Dec. 1, 2007, the Tigers met Tennessee in the SEC's title game. Before the game, all the talk was about head coach Les Miles. Everybody said he was leaving LSU to be the head coach at Michigan. They just knew it.

Miles called a press conference and said he was staying at LSU. Since he did, he was the only one there who knew what was going on.

Except for LSU cornerback Jonathan Zenon.

In the game, Tennessee led 14-13 in the last quarter. When the Volunteers lined up for a play, Zenon couldn't believe what he saw. He knew just what was coming.

Tigers

The UT quarterback sailed a flat pass to Zenon's side. He stepped up and snagged the interception. He then took a joyride right into the end zone for a touchdown. After the two-point conversion, the final score of 21-14 was on the board. The Tigers were SEC champs on their way to the national championship.

Jonathan Zenon just knew something that day the same way you know some things in your life. You know what your favorite subject is in school, what your favorite flavor of ice cream is. You know you're an LSU fan.

Nobody can work it out on paper why you know these things. You just do. That's the way it is with your faith in Jesus. You know that he is God's son and is the savior of the world. You know it with all your heart and soul.

You just know it, and because you know him, Jesus knows you. That is all you really need to know.

List ten things you know for sure about yourself and your life. Shouldn't #1 be "I am a Christian"?

DAY 18

IMPORTANT STUFF

Read Matthew 6:31-34.

Put God's kingdom first in your life.

Pete Maravich found what really mattered.

Maravich is a basketball legend. At LSU, he averaged 44 points a game, still the all-time college record. He holds every Tiger scoring record even though he couldn't play as a freshman and didn't have the three-point line.

Pistol Pete's goal growing up was to "play pro basketball, get a big diamond ring, and make a million dollars." He did all that so he seemed to have it all.

But once Maravich left basketball, his life didn't go too well. He tried everything from yoga to Hinduism to being a vegetarian. He had troubles with alcohol. "My life," he said, "had no meaning at all."

When he was 35, he found the priority for his life he had been hunting. He gave his life to Jesus and became a preacher. He shared his message that through Christ he finally became the man God had always wanted him to be. By putting basketball ahead of God, he had had his priorities wrong.

A priority is what you regard as what's most important in your life. It's what really matters to you. It may not be basketball as Pete Maravich once thought it was, but it's something.

It could be anything, from making good grades to being a cheerleader, to getting to a new level on a video game. It may even be making your parents proud of you.

The big question is whether God is one of your priorities. The truth is he should be first. God said we are to seek him first. Not second or third but first.

In Jesus, God showed you the way you are to do everything. You serve and obey him.

God — and God alone — is No. 1.

Write down ten things that are important to you. Where is God on that list? Talk about how important God is to you.

THE GREATEST

Read Mark 9:33-37.

To be the greatest in God's kingdom, you must put others above yourself and serve them.

LSU has had many great plays in its football history. Only one, though, is the greatest.

On Halloween night 1959, Heisman-Trophy winner Billy Cannon treated LSU fans to the greatest trick ever played on Ole Miss. LSU was ranked No. 1; Ole Miss was No. 3. A fog rolled in, making the whole field look spooky.

Ole Miss led 3-0 with ten minutes left. The Rebels punted and Cannon did something the coaches had told him not to. If the kick went inside the 15-yard line, he was not supposed to touch it but let the ball roll dead.

Instead, Cannon fielded the ball at the 11. What followed was "an incredible, absolutely unbelievable run to glory."

Cannon broke three tackles and then busted though a Rebel mob at the 25. By the time he hit midfield, eight Ole Miss players had had a hand on him! He faked the last tackler out and sailed the rest of the way like a ghost in the fog. That run was the difference. LSU won 7-3.

When you think about being the greatest at something, what do you think of? Probably being better than everybody else, right? You get the highest score on a video game or on a test. You win at tennis or dodge ball at PE.

But Jesus turned being the greatest upside down. He said something really strange. To be the greatest for Jesus, you have to be last. How weird is that? What he meant is that you must put other people first in your life. You always are kind to and help other people.

If you live like that, God is so pleased with you that he names you one of his children. You can't be any greater than that!

Promise yourself that at school
you will seek somebody out
to smile at them and help them.

MAKE SOME MUSIC

Read Psalm 98:4-6.

*Shout to the Lord, burst into song,
and make music.*

At a night game in Tiger Stadium, the noise is so loud that the game isn't just seen, it's heard! The biggest noisemakers of them all are the kids in the LSU Tiger Band.

"The Golden Band from Tigerland" began way back in 1893 as a military band with only eleven members. The group didn't appear at halftime of a football game until 1924.

In the 1930s, Gov. Huey Long decided LSU should have the biggest and best marching band in the country. With the state's help (and money), the band grew to 250 members. It has 325 today.

World War II forced a major change in the band. It had always been nothing but guys, but now there weren't enough of them. For the first time, coeds (female students) became real musicians and not just majorettes.

The band building burned to the ground in 1958. The band lost its uniforms and all the instruments except for one baritone horn and sixteen sousaphones. The band still uses those sousaphones.

Most LSU fans really enjoy hearing the Tiger Marching Band play at a football game. If you like the band and its music, then you have music in your heart, too.

But do you ever let that music come out in praise of God the way it comes out in praise of the Tigers? Do you sing in church, or do you just kind of stand there and mumble a few words? Are you embarrassed to sing?

Music and singing have almost always been a part of worshipping God. Think about this: God loves you and he always will. That should make you sing for joy, especially in church.

Sing your favorite song and your favorite church song. Remember that God likes to hear you sing praises to him.

THE NEW YOU

Read 2 Corinthians 5:15-18.

*The moment you believe in Christ,
you are a new person.*

Glen "Big Baby" Davis was disappointed and mad at himself. So before the 2006-07 basketball season, he made himself over.

LSU's great 2005-06 season ended with a loss in the Final Four. Davis walked off the court after that game knowing that he had not played well. The problem was his body. He had let his weight grow to nearly 340 pounds.

So he changed his eating habits. Gone were the cheeseburgers he loved. Instead, he ate fruits and veggies. Organic oatmeal became his breakfast. "It tastes as nasty as ever," he said. "But you can't eat for taste. You've got to eat for results."

Davis also ran and lifted weights a lot. The result was a complete makeover of his body.

He dropped to 285 pounds for the 2006-07 season. Believe it or not, he was lighter than he had been since the seventh grade.

No longer the "Big Baby" after his makeover, Davis led the league in rebounding and was third in scoring. He was first team All-SEC.

Have you ever seen one of those TV shows where they take someone, buy them some clothes, and redo their hair and makeup? Or a show that puts someone on a diet. It's called a makeover. When it's all done, it makes them look like a new person.

But they're really not a new person. That's because those changes are just on the outside. When you get a haircut or get a new pair of jeans, you're still the same person, aren't you?

If you really want to be a new person, you have to change in the inside, in your heart. The way that is done is with Jesus. You become a new person when you do things to please Jesus and not other people.

List some ways you can change the way you look. Then list some ways you can change how you act with Jesus' help.

SMILING FACES

Read Isaiah 35:5-10.

*Those who find Jesus will also find
joy that lasts forever.*

Reggie Robinson was smiling all over the place. And it was the first day of spring practice, for crying out loud! Players are supposed to hate spring practice!

This was the spring of 2002, and Robinson was a senior wide receiver. He was so happy because he was back on the field. For a while, football had been taken away from him. What took it away was a pizza.

In the fall of 2001, he reached out to hand his son some pizza. He suddenly felt a shock and knew he had hurt his back badly. He had surgery and missed the whole season.

For a while, Robinson wasn't sure he would ever play football again. Then in the spring he was cleared for practice. Still, the injury was on his mind despite all the smiles.

After that first practice, he said he was sore. But then he smiled. "Not from the surgery," he said, but "from having a helmet back on my head." Robinson played in every game but one in 2002 and caught seven passes.

A smile is a wonderful thing. You smile at someone, and it makes them want to smile at you. That's the way a smile works. You give it away and it comes back to you. It seems to make everybody around you happy, like turning on a bright light in a dark room.

And, hey, you have a good reason to walk around with a goofy smile on your face all the time. Not because of a joke you've heard or from anything you've done but because of what God has done for you. The God of everything loves you so much that he died for you on a cross so you would know he loves you.

Now that's something to smile about!

Stand in front of a mirror and make some different smiles. How did you feel? How does your smile make others feel?

ON THE MOVE

Read Colossians 3:8-10.

You have started living a new life.
It is being made new.

Trains, boats planes. Then there's campers, motorcycles, and pickup trucks. Whatever it takes, Tiger fans will use it to hit the road and get to an LSU game.

Short on cash, some 75 LSU cadets hopped a freight train for the game in 1919 against Tulane in New Orleans. But a worker found the moochers and said he would call the police. They managed to talk him into letting them ride on for free and made the game on time.

The cadets even got a free meal since there was some sugar cane aboard the freight train.

Those same cadets rode home in style on a passenger train after LSU pulled off a big 27-6 upset. With their little bit of cash, they had placed a bet on the Tigers and won big.

Tigers

In 1922, fans got to the Tulane game any way they could. A traffic survey in Baton Rouge counted 2,280 automobiles, nine motorcycles, 32 horseback riders, 50 horse-drawn buggies, two bicycles, one tractor, and thirty folks who walked into town. LSU won again 25-14.

Like those LSU fans, most of the trips you take wind up back home. Sometimes, though, you go someplace new for good. Have you ever changed schools? Has your family ever moved to a new place? Even if you haven't moved, you might have thrown away old toys and replaced them with some new ones. Once those changes happen, you can't go back.

And you don't really want to. Meeting new people, new things, and new places is part of growing up. It changes you.

That's the way it is when you give your life to Jesus. He changes you, and he will keep on changing you, making you a better person.

With Jesus, you can never turn back.

Talk about the ways Jesus has changed you. Would you want to go back?

LESSON LEARNED

Read Psalm 143:8-11.

*Teach me what you want me to do
because you are my God.*

A team will often call a timeout when the other team is about to try a field goal. They hope it will make the kicker nervous. One time, though, LSU's kicker called the timeout himself. He had learned a lesson.

Doug Moreau kicked thirteen field goals for the 7-2-1 Bayou Bengals of 1964. At the time, it was a college record.

Moreau had never kicked a field goal until he arrived at LSU. He taught himself by using the telephone line that stretched across his yard at home.

The Tigers wound up in the Sugar Bowl against Syracuse. With 3:48 left, the score was tied at 10, and the Tigers lined up for a 28-yard field goal. Syracuse was out of timeouts, but Moreau surprisingly called one.

Why in the world? "I needed it," he said. He had missed a kick against Miss. State because he also played flanker and had been out of breath when he kicked. "I remembered that and used the timeout to catch my breath."

With the lesson learned, Moreau's kick was good. LSU won 13-10.

You learn lessons at school. Math, science, history, English, a foreign language such as Spanish, computer science. Teachers teach lessons; you learn them. But life outside of school teaches you lessons, too. How to bait a hook. How to dance. Good manners. In every case, somebody teaches you.

And you learn lessons about your faith, too. God set down in his book all you need to know about living a godly life. He even sent Jesus to show you how you are to treat other people.

Just like in the classroom, you need to be a good student to learn God's lessons.

What's your favorite subject?
What about it do you like the most?

BAD TIMES

Read Luke 18:7-8.

*God will make things right one day
for those who follow Jesus.*

Bandon Bass knew some bad times, so he has helped some kids enjoy some good times.

Bass played basketball for LSU for two seasons before he turned pro in 2005. He was the SEC Freshman of the Year in 2004 and the SEC Player of the Year in 2005. He was then drafted into the NBA and became a millionaire.

Bass knew some bad times as a kid growing up. When he was 10, his mother died of a heart attack right in front of him. He lived with his father and then moved in with an aunt.

For a while, he didn't play basketball at all. "All I did was ride my bike all day long," he said. He started playing again when he was 13, but he never got to go to any basketball camps. "Couldn't afford it," he said.

Bass didn't forget those bad times. He has used some of his money to hold basketball camps for kids in Louisiana who can't afford them. "God has blessed me in so many ways," he said. "I've had to go through a lot. I just want to give something back."

Grown-ups sometimes seem to think kids have it easy, that they don't have problems and cares. But children, like adults, do have some bad times, don't they? Like getting sick. Having a friend turn on you and make fun of you. Making a really bad grade on a test.

Life is hard, even if you're a Christian kid. Faith in Jesus Christ doesn't give you a free pass on life's bad times. But faith in Jesus does give you help and strength in getting through them.

You keep the faith. You pray. You trust. You know that someday God will make it right for you. The bad times are not forever; your faith should be.

Recall a time things were bad for you.
Thank God for helping you get through it.

FRUIT TREES

Read Matthew 7:15-20.

A good tree bears good fruit, but a bad tree gives only bad fruit.

Fruit — oranges, that is — came down like rain the night LSU blasted Ole Miss 61-17.

The win on Dec. 5, 1970, wrapped up both the SEC title and a berth in the Orange Bowl for the Tigers. Late in the one-sided game, celebrating LSU students began to pelt the field with hundreds of oranges.

The fired-up students halted the throwdown when the announcer said the Tigers would get a penalty if they didn't stop. But then LSU scored another touchdown — and the oranges started flying again. One hacked off Ole Miss player picked up an orange and sailed it back into the stands towards the happy students.

Everybody said the game would be close, but the Tigers were never in any real trouble.

They led 33-17 after three quarters and then scored four touchdowns in the last period. All-American Tommy Casanova became the first player in SEC history to return two punts for touchdowns in a game.

LSU head coach Charles McClendon called the romp "the most important victory of my life." It was certainly the most fruity.

Just about everybody loves fruit and fruity desserts. What do you like? Apples, grapes, bananas, peaches, mangos? Even the fast food places have fruit pies. A big grocery store has strange fruits you may never have heard of like kumquats. Try saying "kumquat" really fast five times in a row.

But have you ever seen or smelled a piece of rotten fruit? It's awful!

To God, people are a lot like fruit trees. He wants you to produce good fruit. You do that by showing love to others just as Jesus did. You're kind and gentle, and when people see you, they smile. That's good fruit.

Draw a picture of your favorite fruit.

WELCOME HOME

Read 2 Corinthians 5:6-9.

We would really rather be out of our bodies and at home with God.

Its nickname is "Death Valley" because it is where teams' hopes go to die. It's the home of LSU football: Tiger Stadium.

In the 1920s, a completely new LSU campus was built three miles south of Baton Rouge. That included a new football stadium. The stands weren't finished in time for the first game, so part of them were just roped off.

Another problem was that folks couldn't get to the place. There weren't any good roads for cars between Baton Rouge and the new campus. The closest way to go was by train.

The new stadium didn't have any dressing rooms yet. The visitors dressed on the train. The Tigers suited up at their old place and then rode taxis to a building near the stadium.

They walked the rest of the way.

That was the beginning of what is today one of the biggest college football stadiums in the country. It's the home where the Tigers prowl.

When somebody says "home," what do you think about? A house? Your room? Your toys?

But home isn't just a place. More than walls and floors, a home is about people. You are at home when you are with the people you love and the people who love you. That's why it doesn't matter what you live in. What matters is the people you share it with, including God.

Oddly, as a Christian, you spend your whole life as a kid and as a grown-up away from your real home. That's because your real home is with God and Jesus in Heaven. There you will live forever with the people whom you love and who love you most of all.

You'll be home because you'll be with God, and nobody loves you more than God does.

List the different places you have lived.
What was different about each one?
What made them all feel like home?

TRUSTWORTHY

Read Psalm 25:1-3.

My God, I trust in you.

The coach of the other team trusted LSU head man Gaynell Tinsley to keep his word. So the Tigers got a big-time bowl bid.

Sugar Bowl hot shots were in New Orleans for the 1949 Tulane-LSU game to invite Tulane to their bowl game. The Tigers messed up all their plans with a 21-0 upset.

So the Sugar Bowl turned to LSU, but there was a real big problem. Oklahoma was already in the game. Their head coach knew how good the Tigers were and didn't want to play them. Undefeated, Oklahoma simply had nothing to gain by playing a strong LSU team.

But Tinsley wanted the Tigers in that game. The coaches from the two teams talked late into the night trying to make a deal. Finally, Tinsley promised that LSU wouldn't recruit in the state of Oklahoma while he was the head coach. The Oklahoma head coach knew the head Tiger could be trusted, so he agreed to the bowl game. Trust won the day for LSU.

To trust in someone means you believe they will do what they say they will. Without thinking about it, you trust your school teachers to teach you. You trust your Sunday school teachers to believe in God and Jesus. You trust your parents to take good care of you. You trust a doctor to help you get well.

But all these are people; that means they will sometimes let you down. They will make mistakes; your trust in them will fail. (Then there are people — like strangers — that your parents warn you never to trust.)

Is there anyplace you can put your trust knowing it will never fail? Yes. In God you can trust. He keeps his promises; he never lies; he always does what he says he will.

List some things you trust your parents to do for you (like feed you). Talk to your parents about each thing.

GOOD SPORTS

Read Titus 2:6-8.

Set an example: Do what is good.

Tiger fans pulled off a remarkable bit of sportsmanship after the 2003 NCAA base-ball regionals.

Jon Zeringue's walk-off home run in the 11th inning at old Alex Box Stadium won the regional for the Tiger. The thrilling 9-8 win was over the UNC-Wilmington Seahawks.

All through the tournament, LSU fans had bonded with the Seahawks. They cheered for them against Tulane. Many fans mixed LSU gear with Seahawk shirts.

Their season over, the Seahawk players gathered in disappointment. That's when an LSU employee walked over to their dugout and said, "Guys, they'd like you to take a lap." "They" were the LSU fans. The players looked along the baselines in shock. The fans were crowding along the fence chanting "Seahawks" and extending their arms for a high five.

The victory lap is an LSU tradition. Until that day, it had never been offered to an opponent.

So the smiling Seahawks took a victory lap. A little of the sting of their defeat was taken away by the sportsmanship of LSU's fans.

Good sportsmanship means more than just following the rules and not cheating. It means you treat the other players with respect. You don't play dirty. You don't say ugly things to them. You don't try to hurt them.

Believe it or not, the Bible talks about good sportsmanship. It's called the Golden Rule: You treat people the way that you want to be treated by them. You act that way all the time and not just while you're playing a game.

If you follow the Golden Rule in sports, at home, at school, and in all things, then you are living the way Jesus wants you to.

What sports do you play? How do you show good sportsmanship in them? What about off the field?

CHOW DOWN!

Read Genesis 9:1-3.

I now give you everything that lives and moves to eat.

Mike the Tiger once had a food problem. What was to be done about it made LSU students so mad they threw campus leaders into a cage and paraded them around the grounds.

World War II cut into Mike's diet. Because of meat rationing, his steak was replaced by what was called "scrap beef." Actually, it was nothing but horse meat and cereal.

Plans were made to move Mike to the zoo in New Orleans. They had plenty of meat there in cold storage. But this was the home of Tulane, LSU's most bitter rival at the time.

The students didn't like it one bit. They were so riled up they kidnapped the student body president and the vice-president. They locked both of them in Mike's traveling cage and pushed them around campus.

But then the reason for sending Mike to New Orleans changed from getting food to getting a little Mikey. He was getting old and time was running out for him to be the father of a baby tiger. Told that, the students gave in.

Like Mike, Americans really do love food. We love to eat all sorts of different things, from hamburgers to chicken, pizza to ice cream. We even have TV channels that talk about food all the time. They show people how to make new dishes for their family to try and eat.

Food is one of God's really good ideas. Isn't it amazing to think that from one apple seed, an entire tree full of apples can grow and give you yummy fruit year after year?

God created this system that lets all living things grow and nourish one another. Your food comes from God and nowhere else. The least you can do is thank him for it.

Three questions to answer: What's your favorite food? What can you cook? Do you always thank God before you eat?

PIONEER SPIRIT

Read Luke 5:4-11.

*They pulled their boats on shore
and left everything to follow Jesus.*

Officially, women's basketball began at LSU in 1975-76. The true pioneers, however, first took the court a long time before that.

The LSU men's basketball program began on Jan. 30, 1909. The first game was played "in a poor lighted hall in Covington." Only a handful of spectators bothered to show up.

That first-ever game was a success, though. The LSU boys were underdogs because the game was played indoors under the lights. They had practiced outdoors the whole time.

But the rookies pulled off a 35-20 defeat of Dixon Academy. They went on to a 5-2 record that first season.

The guys weren't the only pioneers in 1909. LSU's coeds also fielded a team. The school yearbook, called the *Gumbo*, didn't pay much attention to the women. It just said they were "only defeated once."

So LSU women's basketball actually began 66 years before the Lady Tigers' media guide says it did.

A pioneer is a person or group, like those LSU women in 1909, who is the first to do something or to try something no one else has done before. The disciples who gave up fishing to follow Jesus were pioneers.

Being a pioneer is scary, but it's also fun. Learning something new in school, going to a new place on vacation, riding a new ride at the fair — it's exciting!

God wants you to go to new places and to try new things for him. He wants you to follow him no matter what. After a while, you get really good at being a Christian and then you can help others become pioneers for Jesus.

On a note card, list some things you can do for God. Decorate it and carry it with you all day as a reminder.

DAY 32

GIVING UP

Read Numbers 13:25-28, 30-32.

Some men said, "We can't attack those people because they are bigger and stronger than we are."

Jerry Stovall got no sympathy when he told his dad he was quitting football at LSU. So he changed his mind and LSU football history.

A freshman in 1959, Stovall looked around at LSU and saw "there were lots of bigger, faster, stronger players than me." So he called his dad to say he was coming home. Dad told him that was just fine; he'd find Jerry a job.

That made the son stop and think. His dad was a salesman who climbed out of bed every day at 5 a.m. He worked from dawn to dusk to keep food on the table.

"There wasn't a whole lot of sympathy there," Jerry said. His father must have been a little hacked off at him for complaining about how hard it was to play a game.

So Jerry told his dad he'd stick with football a little longer. He never thought about quitting again and became an All-American running back. He was LSU's head football coach from 1980-83 and is a member of the hall of fame.

Everybody feels like quitting at some time or another. Maybe that sport at school is harder than you thought it was. Maybe you just can't figure out math. Maybe you and a friend just don't get along anymore.

Quitting is easy. But when it comes to God, remember the story of the people of Israel. They quit when the Promised Land was theirs for the taking. They forgot that God would never, ever give up on them.

God never quits on you either. So you must never give up on God even if it seems like your prayers aren't getting through. You just don't know what God may be up to. The only way to find out is to never quit on God.

Winners never quit; quitters never win.
How does this apply to God and you?

WELL, EXCUSE ME!

Read Luke 9:59-62.

If you start to follow Jesus and then make excuses not to serve him, you are not fit for Heaven.

How about this excuse for losing a game: The players were spending too much time on their studies!

The football seasons way back in 1897 and '88 were pretty much wiped out by a yellow fever epidemic. It was so bad anyone wishing to enter or leave Baton Rouge had to get a permit. All the mail was disinfected.

By 1900, football was back in full swing. The team smashed Millsaps College 70-0 but then lost to Tulane 29-0. Some unhappy fans came up with two excuses for the big loss.

The first one was "overconfidence" because LSU had gotten used to "running through Tulane's teams in the past without any effort."

The second excuse is one that you can bet won't be heard around campus today. The local paper said the team lost because the players had been "doing such splendid class work" they hadn't had enough time to practice.

You've made some excuses before, haven't you? What excuse did you use when you didn't do your homework? Or your chores? Have you ever said you felt bad so you didn't have to do something you didn't want to?

Lots of folks make excuses when we don't like the way things are going. Or when stuff gets too hard. Or we fail at something.

We do it with our faith life, too. We say the Bible's too hard to read. The weather's too pretty to be shut up in church. Or praying in public is downright embarrassing.

But, you know, Jesus died for you without making any excuses. The least you can do is live for him with no excuses.

What excuse did you use the last time you missed church? Do you think God thought it was a good one?

DAY 34

JUST PERFECT

Read Matthew 5:43-48.

Jesus said, "Be perfect, just as God is perfect."

Once upon a time, LSU played what a sportswriter said was a perfect game. They had to.

Pretty much everybody was surprised when the Tigers received an invitation to the 1966 Cotton Bowl. They were 7-3 and had lost badly twice. They had to play Arkansas, which had won 22 straight games.

"The Tigers were hopelessly outmatched," said LSU head coach Charles McClendon.

Sure enough, Arkansas took the opening kickoff and scored. Then the Tigers shocked everyone by marching 87 yards to tie it at 7-7.

After a Razorback fumble, LSU used five straight running plays from the 19 to score a second touchdown. The Tigers led 14-7 at halftime. The defense took over after that, and

the 14-7 score held up.

The head coach called it. "We didn't make a mistake," he said. To pull off one of the biggest upsets in LSU history, the Tigers were perfect.

Nobody's always perfect. That means you never do anything wrong, you never make a mistake, you never do anything clumsy. Ever.

Oh, you can be perfect now and then. Like on a test. Or playing a song on an instrument. But you're not perfect all the time. Only one man was ever perfect. And that was Jesus.

But yet Jesus commands you to be perfect. Didn't we just say that was impossible? Has Jesus got it wrong?

Nope, not at all. When Jesus spoke of being perfect, he talked of loving perfectly as God does. To love perfectly is to love all others and not just those whom you like or who do nice things for you.

To love perfectly is to love everyone.

List three folks it's really hard for you to love. Then list something good about each one. Try to love them for that.

KEEP IT SIMPLE

Read 1 John 1:5-10.

If we admit to God that we have sinned, he will forgive us.

Basketball is the silliest game in the world" because there's only one ball. "If I have the ball who can beat me?"

That was the simple, winning formula of the first LSU basketball player to be an All-America. He was Malcolm "Sparky" Wade. He showed up in Baton Rouge in 1931 "with a dollar in his pocket and some sandwiches wrapped in an old [handkerchief]." He didn't look like a basketball player; he was only 5'6" tall.

But he had that simple formula. He worked himself into the player who could control the ball. He became "a super showman" long before Pistol Pete Maravich. He could shoot, pass and do just about anything with a basketball, "including dance on it."

Tigers

There was no NCAA Tournament in those days, so the Tigers played Pittsburgh after the season in a national title game. Pitt put two and three guys on Wade the whole game. He couldn't score, but he could still control the ball. So he did. He spent the night passing to his teammates and LSU won 41-37.

Being a kid isn't simple. You have to juggle school and homework, baseball or basketball, church and Sunday school, dancing class, 4-H, and anything else that comes along. You have to do your chores at the house like making up your bed and taking out the garbage.

But, you know, life is really pretty simple. Just like Sparky Wade showed with the game of basketball. Put the basic stuff first. Worship God, love your family, honor your teachers, and always do your best.

That's means you're obeying God in the way you live. It's simple — and it's the best.

***It's simple: Ask God for forgiveness
of our sins and we get it.
Why do you think God made it so easy?***

SOUND OFF!

Read Revelation 5:11-13.

*I heard thousands and thousands
of angels singing.*

One night in Baton Rouge, the LSU crowd was so loud it made the earth move.

It happened on Oct. 8, 1988, against the Auburn Tigers. Auburn led 6-0. With 1:47 left in the game, LSU quarterback Tommy Hodson threw a touchdown pass to his tailback, Eddie Fuller, for the 7-6 win. The fans made so much noise it registered as an earthquake in LSU's Geology Department.

The noise showed up on a seismograph, a device used to record and measure earthquakes. "It was a total surprise," said one of LSU's research assistants.

Some folks have said the story is a myth. But it showed up in the Ripley's Believe or Not Museum in New York. On display was a photo of the seismograph reading.

LSU geology professors agree it was the fans' jumping up and down that showed up on the seismograph. However they did it, Tiger fans made the earth move that night

You may not have ever heard a racket loud enough to cause an earthquake, but you're used to a lot of noise, aren't you? Your school is noisy, especially at PE and between classes. Football, basketball, and soccer games are noisy. Car horns blow, dogs bark, TV's shout.

You live in a noisy world. It's fun, but if you let it, all that noise will drown out the gentle voice of God in your heart. That means you need some quiet time every day. You can say your prayers, talk to God, and then listen for what he may have to say to you.

Much about Heaven will be strange, but one thing will make you feel right at home. As the Bible says, it's a noisy place. That's because everybody's whooping it up for God.

Get a watch to time yourself. Stay quiet and think about God for three minutes.

BRAG ABOUT IT!

Read Job 38:8-12.

Have you ever commanded the morning to come?

A coach bragged one time that those LSU boys didn't stand a chance against his team.

The Tigers made their first-ever road trip way back in 1894. They traveled by steamboat. In 1939, they became one of the first teams to fly to a football game. They flew to Massachusetts to play Holy Cross. Few of the players had flown before, and several got airsick.

LSU Head coach Bernie Moore didn't like the flying too much. It didn't help his nerves any when a senior guard majoring in engineering calculated it would take 32 seconds to hit the ground if the plane's engines quit.

The Holy Cross coach bragged that he might start his second team against LSU. He said his bunch would show those Southern boys the way football was supposed to be played.

Senior end Ken Kavanaugh was one of the players who got sick on the plane. (He was an Air Force pilot in World War II.) He got well really quick and scored four touchdowns. LSU beat Holy Cross easily 28 7.

So much for all that bragging.

Grown-ups like to brag about what they've done. Like putting up buildings, running for office, and buying new houses and cars. You may brag, too, about your grades, your video games, or the soccer goals you've scored.

But it all makes God laugh. We are nothing compared to God. We brag about space flight; God hung the moon, the planets, and the stars in the heavens he created. A TV weatherman guesses at the weather; God commands it. You work hard to learn math and science; God takes care of the whole universe.

You and everyone else do have one thing worth bragging about for sure: God loves you.

List three things God can brag about.
Brag to somebody that God loves you.

DAY 38

HANG IN THERE

Read Mark 14:32-36.

Jesus prayed, "Father, not what I want but what you want."

The 2000 season was on the line. And the LSU softball team struck out 21 times and didn't score a run for 12 innings. But they kept hanging in there.

On May 20 at Tiger Park, LSU met Southern Mississippi in a softball regional. A loss meant the season was over for the SEC champs. They HAD to win this game. What happened was "nearly 4¹/² hours of unspeakable drama."

The innings slipped by — five, six, seven — and neither team could score. Eight, nine, ten. Still no score. Finally, the home-plate ump asked LSU catcher Jennnifer Schuelke, "How long are you going to let this go?" She said, "As long as it takes."

In other words, the Tigers would hang in

there, and that is what they did. In the top of the thirteenth inning, the Tigers scored. All-American Stephanie Hastings hit a sacrifice fly to drive the game's first and last run home.

Southern Miss then loaded the bases. But the Tigers got a pair of strike-outs to end the game — with a school-record 59th win.

Being a champion is never easy. It's always hard. Quitting is heaps easier. But the only way to be a champion is to never give up, never quit. You've got to hang in there.

It's just a fact that life beats you up sometimes. Just expect it and keep going.

That's what Jesus did. On that awful night in the garden, he begged God to not make him die on the cross. But he gave in to what God wanted him to do. He hung in there.

Jesus is our example. Following God's will for your life as Jesus did is sometimes hard. But you can win because God is with you.

Talk about something you did one time that was really hard. Did you think about quitting? Why didn't you?

SIZE MATTERS

Read Luke 19:1-10.

*Zacchaeus wanted to see Jesus,
but he was so short, he had to
climb a tree.*

Dalton Hilliard was just too small to be a big-time running back. Or so they said.

College recruiters took one look at his size and backed off. He was 5'8" tall and weighed 185 pounds. When Hilliard showed up in Baton Rouge in 1982, even LSU's coaches wondered if he were too small to carry the ball. The linebackers coach ended the argument. He said, "An offensive line opens holes that are wide, not high."

The backfield coach soon told head coach Jerry Stovall the team had a problem. He said, "Our third-string back is better than anyone we have." That third-stringer was Hilliard.

In the fall of 1982, this player who was too

small became the first freshman running back in LSU history to start. The player nicknamed "Little Big Man" went on to become LSU's all-time leading rusher and leading scorer.

Dalton Hilliard's size just didn't matter.

Everybody seems to think bigger is better. Bigger houses, bigger burgers. You even super-size your fries. You just can't wait to grow up some so you can be taller and bigger, can you?

But, you know, size didn't matter to Jesus. Salvation came to the house of a bad man who was so short he had to climb a tree to even see Jesus. Zacchaeus was a big shot because he was rich, but that didn't matter to Jesus either. Zacchaeus was saved because he was sorry for all the wrong things he had done, and he changed his life as a result.

The same is true for you. What matters to Jesus is the size of your heart, the one you give to him.

**_Look at some of your old pictures.
Have you grown much?
Have you grown in your love for Jesus?_**

GET TO WORK

Read Matthew 9:35-38.

There are only a few workers.

He was so bad his quarterback couldn't believe he was coming to LSU. Yet he left Baton Rouge as a two-time All-America. How in the world? Hard work.

Wendell Davis was not really a hot prospect receiver out of high school. The LSU coach who signed him said Davis "looked like a normal little guy." LSU quarterback Tommy Hodson worked out with him, and Davis couldn't catch his passes. "I was not impressed," he said.

Davis didn't have the greatest raw talent in the world, but he had something else. He was a hard worker. On campus, he worked tirelessly at catching footballs and running the right routes. He worked on his hand-eye coordination. He got faster. Soon, everything thrown his way was sticking to his hands.

Tigers

Davis got the start as a redshirt freshman in 1986. Hodson right away knew Davis was his go-to receiver. He had 80 catches in '86, the most in the country. He left LSU as both the school's and the SEC's all-time leading receive. He was a first-round draft pick.

All because he worked hard for everything.

When grown-ups talk about what they do for a living, they're talking about their job. Work is just a part of life. How about you? Do you work hard or hardly work? Even now, you maybe can earn a little bit of pocket money by doing your chores or by helping your mom or your dad around the house or out in the yard.

There's another kind of work you can do right now and all your life. You can work for God. Jesus said there are only a few people willing to work for God. That's still true, even today. God needs more people to work for him. God needs you.

So what are you waiting for?

Come up with some ways you can work for God right now. Get to work.

DAY 41

A CONFUSED MESS

Read Genesis 11:1-9.

The Lord mixed up the language of the whole world there.

LSU football was just one confused mess.

Back in 1916, the head coach was fired in mid-season. The fans didn't like it, and the whole team threatened to quit. The coach who had been fired showed up at a team meeting; he told the Tigers to keep playing and they did.

Assistant coach Irving Pray took over, but he was on a boat to Cuba when the team played a game. He was a sugar chemist; he had already promised to sail to Cuba when the sugar-cane season started. Pray led the Tigers to a 17-7 win over Arkansas. After that, he hopped on a boat the day of the Miss. State game (a 13-3 win).

LSU officials then scrambled around and borrowed an assistant coach from Texas. He kind of straightened out some of the confusion when he coached the rest of the season.

LSU hired a new coach for 1917, but confusion soon set in again. He left after one season.

The story of the Tower of Babel shows that there is confusion when something is going on that God doesn't like. You see, God likes order. When he created everything, he took confusion and gave it order. With God, there is right and there is wrong. There is a way people should live.

There's a whole bunch of confused people in the world today. You may know some kids at school who can't figure things out. Like how they should act. Or treat other kids and their teachers. People's lives are a confused mess when they live in a way that isn't God's way.

With God there is order in your life. You know what to do. Without God, there is confusion in your life. You have no clue.

Make a mess in your room. This is your life without God. Clean up the mess. This is your life with God.

ON CALL

Read 1 Samuel 3:1-10.

Samuel said, "Speak, Lord. I'm listening."

At first, Joseph Barksdale didn't like the idea one bit, but he answered his coach's call.

Barksdale was a defensive tackle. In 2007, he came to Baton Rouge to be a football star.

His first day on campus, he meet the offensive line coach. He asked Barksdale if he had ever thought of playing on the offensive line. "Absolutely not" was the answer.

But he could see that the team was short on that side of the line. Head coach Les Miles was an old offensive lineman himself, so he had a little chat with Barksdale.

The coach told him he could be a star if he worked hard. Barksdale liked that, so he answered the call and made the move.

The first thing he learned was that o-linemen

had to be really good athletes. Unlike the defense, he said, "You have to be consistent and you can't take any plays off."

Barksdale became a starter at right tackle.

You may have answered the call when a coach needed you to play a new position In a game as Joseph Barksdale did. Or when your teacher calls on you to answer a question. Or your dad asks you to help him mow the lawn.

Did you know God, too, is calling you? God wants you to do something for him with your life. That sounds scary, doesn't it?

But answering God's call doesn't mean you have to be a preacher. Or be a missionary in some way-off place where they never heard of Cajun food or the LSU Tigers.

God calls you to serve him right where you are. At school. At home. On the playground. You answer God's call when you do everything for his glory and not your own.

Talk and pray with your parents about
the call God might be placing on your life
and how you can answer it.

DAY 43

TICK TOCK

Read Matthew 25:1-13.

*Stay alert. You don't know the day
or the hour when Jesus will return.*

LSU head football coach Paul Dietzel (1955-61) didn't operate in the same time zone as everyone else.

Dietzel made sure every detail was covered. His schedule for game day even had a space that allowed five minutes for "NP." The players knew this meant "nervous pee."

One August, Dietzel had a team meeting set for 1:05 p.m. Linebacker Steve Ward took a nap in his room and woke up at 1 o'clock. He hurried to the meeting room and looked at his watch as he arrived: exactly 1:05.

Dietzel himself opened the door. Ward said, "Coach, my watch shows it's 1:05." The head coach said, "Son, I don't recognize your time. I operate on Central Dietzel Time and you're three minutes late. See me after this meeting."

Ward had to run three miles after practice for the next three days. "I was never late again," to a team meeting, he said. Even after he left LSU, Ward kept his watch three minutes fast and operated on Central Dietzel Time.

Even though you're a kid, the clock has a lot to do with your life. You have to be at school on time or you're headed for big trouble. Athletic events, classes, church, even birthday parties — they all start at a certain time. You probably have a bedtime on school nights.

All that time, every second of your life, is a gift from God since he's the one who dreamed up time in the first place.

So what does God consider making good use of the time he gives us? As Jesus' story tells us, it's being ready for the wonderful and glorious day when Jesus will return.

When will that be? Only time will tell.

Count to sixty but not real fast.
That's a minute. Any minute now
Jesus could come back.

WHAT YOU WEAR

Read Genesis 37:1-5.

His father made Joseph a pretty coat, and his brothers hated him.

LSU quarterback Y.A. Tittle is the only Tiger player ever to moon the other team and still make the Hall of Fame.

Tittle led the Tigers from 1945-47. The 1946 team went 9-1, finished in the top ten, and tied Arkansas in the Cotton Bowl.

Against Ole Miss in 1947, Tittle played cornerback on defense and intercepted a pass. The Rebel receiver managed to reach out and grab at Tittle's uniform before he ran away. His belt buckle gave way and so did his pants.

Tittle suddenly had a real problem. He had to run 70 yards through Ole Miss tacklers. But he also had to do it while holding the ball in one hand and his pants in the other.

One Rebel player said, "I was racing down

the field after him laughing. I couldn't help it. It was just the funniest thing I ever saw in football."

Before Tittle's pants wound up around his ankles, he was knocked out of bounds. "I'm not sure if I could have scored," he said.

You dress a certain way for school and for church. How silly would it be to wear shoes and a coat into a swimming pool?

Your clothes wear out and you outgrow them. So you change clothes all the time. Getting a new pair of shoes or some new jeans changes the way you look. It doesn't change you, does it? You're still the same person.

Do you think Jesus cares about the clothes you wear? What he cares about is your heart. What he cares about is how you act. It doesn't matter whether you're wearing clothes fit for a king or rags a homeless person might wear.

Clothes don't make you the person you are. Loving Jesus does.

Dress up in a wild outfit.
In front of a mirror, act out what Jesus would say to you if he saw you.

YOU NEVER KNOW

Read Exodus 3:7-12.

Moses asked God, "Who am I to go before Pharaoh?" God answered, "I will be with you."

You just never know what might happen in a football game. Take that national championship battle of Jan. 4, 2004.

LSU and everybody else spent the 2003 football season in mighty Oklahoma's shadow. They were ranked No. 1 all season. Their quarterback won the Heisman Trophy. They had the best defense in college ball.

Everybody said the Bayou Bengals didn't stand a chance in the BCS title game. Heck, Oklahoma even offered for sale on its web site some stuff declaring them national champs — before the game!

The Sooners had one really big problem: They hadn't played LSU. When they did, the

Tigers

Tigers turned college football upside down.

On the first play, LSU tailback Justin Vincent — the game's MVP — busted a 64-yard run to the OU 16. The message was clear: LSU was not afraid and Oklahoma should be.

LSU won 21-14. You just never know.

In your life, you never know what is gonna happen. Or what you can do until you try. You may think you can't play football, cook supper, or run the lawn mower. But have you tried?

Your parents sometimes tell you to do some things you think you can't do. God is the same way. You just never know what God is going to ask you to do. Moses sure didn't. Can you sing a solo in church? Tell someone else about Jesus? Go on a mission trip?

You may think, "I can't do that." But if it's something God wants you to do, you can. You just have to trust him. With God's help, you can do it.

Think of something you've never tried before but would like to. Decide to do it and pray for God to help you.

WILD AND CRAZY

Read Acts 4:13-14.

The leaders realized Peter and John were ordinary men. That surprised them.

What LSU head basketball coach Dale Brown did gave Tiger fans one of the wildest and craziest college basketball games ever.

On Feb. 3, 1990, Loyola Marymount played the Tigers in Baton Rouge. LMU was "the freak show of college basketball." They were the run-and-gun team of all time; their goal was to get a shot up in four or five seconds! They averaged an incredible 121 points a game!

The only way to beat them was to slow them down, right? Brown didn't see it that way. With his lineup that included Shaquille O'Neal, he figured the Tigers could run with LMU.

More than 14,000 LSU fans showed up, like folks "at the state fair lining up to see the three-headed calf."

They saw a circus. The scoring came so fast that an electric typewriter used to record the action (This was before computers.) caught fire when the motor burned up.

LSU won the wild and crazy game 148-141.

Sports like basketball do sometimes get wild and crazy, don't they? Did you know that Jesus calls you to a wild and crazy life? One that is full of adventure like Peter and John had.

Chances are, though, that you think church is boring most of the time. That's because you are not being wild and crazy for Jesus.

Jesus doesn't want you to sit around. He wants you to get up and get out. Sing in a choir. Ride your bike with a Jesus tag on it. Go to Christian camps. Help old folks when you get the chance. Pray for other kids.

Being a Christian isn't supposed to be dull. It should be wild and crazy.

With your parents' help, come up with a wild and crazy thing or two you can do for Jesus. Then do them.

THE PRIZE

Read Philippians 3:10-14.

The heavenly prize is Jesus himself.

College football players win all kinds of honors and awards. But an LSU player once got an offer that has never been made since. He was to be made a Louisiana state senator!

LSU halfback "Miracle" Abe Mickal led the Tigers to a 23-4-5 record from 1933-35. He is in the College Football Hall of Fame.

Louisiana Gov. Huey Long was a big fan. He often visited practice and helped Mickal take off his jersey. He wanted to make Mickal a state senator, which made LSU head coach Biff Jones really mad. He told his athletic director Long was hurting his team's morale by making such a big deal out of one player.

So Long had another idea. He'd make state senators of the whole team!

Mickal refused to report to be sworn in. The

athletic director finally ended the whole mess. He told the governor if Mickal were made a state senator, he would be ruled ineligible for football. The $10 per day he would be paid meant he would now be a pro, not an amateur.

Hey, we like awards and prizes don't we? A trophy from your baseball or softball team. A certificate for good grades or perfect attendance. A medal for something good you did. Isn't it cool to have your picture in the paper?

We all like other people to notice when we have worked hard and have done a good job.

But you have to be real careful that you don't start worshipping your prizes and bragging about them. That means they become idols.

The greatest prize of all won't rust, fade, or collect dust. It's the only one worth winning. It's eternal life through Jesus Christ, and God gives it to you for trusting in Jesus.

Rank all the prizes you've won in order of how important they are to you. Compare each one to the prize of being a child of God for believing in Jesus.

HOMELESS

Read Matthew 8:19-22.

Jesus said, "I have no place to call home with a bed to sleep in."

The homeless Tigers once played a home football game 1,400 miles from Baton Rouge.

In September 2005, the LSU football team also endured the chaos and sorrow brought on by Hurricane Katrina. They had to start their season two weeks later than they had planned. Even then, they traveled across the country to Tempe, Ariz., to play a game originally set for Tiger Stadium.

"We wanted to win for our fans," said senior Skyler Green. He had shared his apartment with relatives and friends who were homeless.

The Sun Devils were gracious hosts. They helped pay LSU's expenses, so more money could go to hurricane relief. They let the Tigers wear their white home jerseys and enter the stadium last. The hotel where the team stayed even came up with a recipe for grits!

With 1:23 left in the game, JaMarcus Russell hit Early Doucet with a touchdown pass and a 35 31 win for the home folks.

You've probably seen them hanging around. That guy with a beard and a backpack holding a sign at the interstate exit. A woman pushing a shopping cart loaded with bags of clothes. They're probably dirty and they smell bad.

You don't know what their story is. They may be women and children running from abuse. Or army veterans haunted by what they saw in a war. They may be sick or injured workers.

They are the homeless. They have nowhere to live and nowhere to sleep at night.

But Jesus calls you to show them mercy, not to hate them. After all, you serve a Lord — your Jesus — who, like them, had no home.

The homeless, too, are God's children.

Talk to your parents about a way you can help the homeless in your town. Then do it.

DREAM WORLD

Read Joshua 3:13-17.

The priests stood on dry ground in the river until all the people had crossed into the Promised Land.

Only two months before his childhood dream came true with a home run, Warren Morris wasn't sure he'd ever play baseball again.

Morris grew up dreaming of winning a championship with a home run. That's what he did with two out in the bottom of the ninth inning in the 1996 College World Series championship game. His two-run homer gave LSU a 9-8 win and the national title.

Much of the season had been a nightmare for Morris. Early on, he hurt his hand. He tried to come back, but the pain just got worse. A pre-season All-America, he was on the bench.

No one could figure out what was wrong. "I wasn't sure I would [ever] play again," he said.

So Morris dropped to his knees one night and prayed, "God, if baseball is what you want me to do in life, then I will do it. [If not], I'll do it and serve you in that way."

Two days later, a doctor found a broken bone in his hand. Morris had surgery and soon was on his way to making his dream come true.

Even at your age, you probably dream about some things. What you want to be when you grow up. Or maybe you dream about being a high school football, basketball, or soccer star.

If your dreams are to come true, you must be sure they're good enough for God. He calls you to do great things for him, and no dream is too big for God. The Israelites could only dream of having their own country for a home — until God made it possible.

You must work hard to make your dreams come true. Give them your best. Just make sure God is there with you and that they're good enough for God to help them come true.

Make a list of your dreams. Talk to your parents about how they can come true.

ANIMAL CRACKERS

Read Psalm 139:1-6, 13-14.

*I praise God because of the
wonderful way you made me.*

Mike the tiger is the most fearsome mascot in the country. But LSU could easily have become known as the Pelicans. Not quite as ferocious, huh?

LSU's first mascot was a greyhound named Drum. That same year, 1896, the football players had pelicans sewn on their jackets. Even so, bit by bit that year, the team came to be called the Tigers.

The football team took the name from the Seventh Louisiana Infantry of the Civil War. They were known to charge with nothing but knives. They also returned from battle wearing necklaces made from Yankee body parts!

The first live cat mascot was a jaguar in 1924. He was nicknamed "Little Eat 'Em Up,"

Tigers

but he didn't last long. He spent most of his time being afraid of all the noise.

In 1936, a student named Mike Chambers, said LSU should have a live mascot. The students raised $750 and bought a tiger cub from the Little Rock Zoo. He was named "Mike" in honor of the guy who came up with the idea.

We respect and admire animals such as Mike, don't we? Isn't it fun on a trip to spot wild turkeys or deer in the woods? A zoo is one of the most fun places in the world to visit. Who in the world could dream up an alligator, a moose, an ostrich, or a tiger?

Well, God dreamed them all up, just like he did the pelican, and the rattlesnake. And just like he dreamed up you.

You are special. You are one of a kind, personally made by God. If you wore a label like the one you have on your shirts, it might say: "Lovingly handmade in Heaven by #1 — God."

***How special does it make you feel to
know that God himself made you?
Share that feeling with your parents.***

DAY 51

DRY SPELL

Read 1 Kings 16:29-30; 17:1; 18:1.

Elijah told Ahab, "There won't be any rain for the next few years."

The long dry spell for LSU football was over.

On Nov. 6, 1982, No. 10 LSU beat No. 7 Alabama 20-10. For eleven seasons in a row, the Tide and Bear Bryant had beaten LSU.

The long drought ended thanks partly to "a feeble-looking, yet heady player named Alan Risher." On this night, he pulled off "miracle after miracle with his right arm and wiggly feet." He completed twenty passes and got yardage all game long by scrambling.

LSU's Jerry Stovall said it was "the biggest victory I've ever had as a coach." He added, "You can't understand what it's like to get hit in the mouth 11 years in a row." Bryant called it "the best beating we've had since the 1960s."

The Tigers ripped off 17 points in the second

quarter. The Tide rallied to cut the lead to 17-10. The Tigers then went on a long drive that ended in a field goal and the 20-10 final score.

The drought was over.

If you live in Louisiana or other parts of the South, you know a little something about drought, don't you? It gets really hot down here, and sometimes in the summer you probably don't get a whole lot of rain in your hometown unless there's a tropical storm or hurricane kicking around somewhere.

The sun bakes everything, including the concrete that gets so hot it burns your feet. Ever seen a dirty truck with "Wash Me" written on the back windshield? It's kind of funny.

God put in you a physical thirst for water to keep you alive. But he also put a spiritual thirst in you. Without God, we are like a dried-up pond. There's no life, only death.

There's only one fountain to go to and drink all you want of the true water of life: Jesus.

**Fill an empty water bottle with sand
to remind you how a soul looks
without God: all dried up and dead.**

DAY 52

A GENTLE MAN

Read John 2:13-16.

Jesus made a whip out of cords and drove the animals and the money changers out of the temple.

He was called "a great model of a Christian gentleman." He was LSU's Harry Rabenhorst.

"Coach Raby" arrived in Baton Rouge in 1925. He coached basketball and baseball and was an assistant football coach. He later served as LSU's athletic director.

Rabenhorst won 344 basketball games, the school record until Dale Brown came along and broke it. He won a national title in basketball and two SEC titles in baseball.

One player said that Coach Raby "was the most pure Christian-type person you'd ever want to meet in life." He was a man who never cheated, who always did what was right. He never asked a professor to change a student's grade. He expected all "his boys" to play by the rules.

How could such a gentleman be so successful? He believed in discipline. He once left a baseball player in Mississippi when the player didn't get to the bus on time after a meal. Coach Raby kept going even though the player came running after the departing bus.

Like Coach Raby, a gentleman is kind, polite, and nice to other people. He isn't mean to others and always tries to do the right thing. Jesus was a gentleman and acted like one.

But as Jesus showed that day in the temple, being a gentleman doesn't mean you're weak. It means you stand up for what is right. At school, you protect those who are weaker than others, who are being bullied.

God is a gentleman, too. He could bully you and boss you around. Instead, he gently asks for your attention and waits for your answer.

Talk to your dad or granddad about how a gentleman acts. Decide if that is how God wants you to act.

NIGHTFALL

Read Psalm 74:15-17.

You rule over the day and the night.

There's just nothing else in college football like Saturday night in Tiger Stadium.

Night football in Death Valley began in 1931. Exactly why it started is not known for sure. Maybe to miss the heat of day games. Or to avoid conflicts with Tulane and Loyola, the other state powerhouses at the time. Or to give fans more chances to see the Tigers play.

Officials expected attendance to go up, but it didn't happen at the first game. It rained.

The opponent was Spring Hill, so it wasn't a big-time game to begin with. Fearing a lot of empty seats, LSU folks dropped ticket prices to $1.50 for reserved sideline seats. It was 75 cents for end zone bleacher seats, and high school students got in for a quarter. Younger

Tigers

students could see the game for just one thin dime. It didn't work. Only about 5,000 fans sat in the rain to watch LSU win 35-0.

Today, Saturday night in Death Valley is "the freaklest, funkiest" place in all of college football.

The light for LSU's night football is artificial, made by man, not God. Our lights can shine on only a part of God's night. They can never chase all of it away. The night, like the day, is a natural part of God's creation.

God made it so you can get some rest and get ready for tomorrow. But it's also fun sometimes, isn't it? Hide and seek is a lot better at night. So is football in Death Valley. God must have had high school football in mind when he made Friday nights.

From the reds and oranges of a sunset to the star-studded dark of midnight — God's night is beautiful. It's a special gift for you.

You think God's night is dead and quiet?
Go outside tonight and listen.
List all the things you hear.

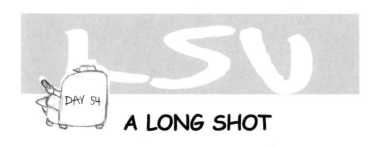

A LONG SHOT

Read Matthew 9:9-10.

*Jesus said, "Follow me," and
Matthew got up and did it.*

One of LSU's greatest football players was once a long shot to even walk. Forget about football.

Defensive tackle Glenn Dorsey was a two-time All-America (2006 and 2007). In 2007, he won three of college football's major awards. All the while, he played with a slight bow to his legs. It was a reminder of a time when he couldn't walk.

When he was 3, Glenn was so bowlegged that doctors told his mother his legs wouldn't straighten up on their own. He couldn't walk for tripping over his own feet.

So his mother fitted him with corrective shoes and ankle braces connected by a bar. The result was a painful memory. Glenn had to sit while his friends played. He took a football to bed at night and dreamed of playing.

By age 8, his legs were straight enough for him to play. He wasn't a long shot anymore.

A long shot is someone or some team that doesn't stand a good chance of doing something. You're a pretty long shot to get married soon or to be named LSU's head track coach.

Matthew was a long shot to become one of Jesus' close friends. He was a tax collector, which meant he was pretty much a crook. He got rich by bullying and stealing from his own people, his own neighbors.

Yet, Jesus said only two words to this lowlife: "Follow me." And Matthew did it.

Like Matthew, we're all long shots to get to Heaven because we can't stand before God with pure, clean hearts. Not unless we do what Matthew did: Get up and follow Jesus. Then we become a sure thing.

Name five things that are long shots in your life (like becoming president). Then name five things that are sure shots (like going to bed tonight).

MIDDLE OF NOWHERE

Read Genesis 28:10-16.

Jacob woke up and said to himself, "The Lord is in this place, and I didn't even know it."

Sue Gunter found fame and fortune at LSU, but she started out pretty much in the middle of nowhere.

The 2010 census listed the population of Walnut Grove, Miss., as 1,911. And that's after the area prison was taken into the city limits.

As late as 2000, the town had 488 people. That's where Gunter grew up playing basketball with her cousins on the family farm. There wasn't anything else to do. "If you were going to be popular," she said, "you better play basketball. Or at least learn to dribble."

Gunter dribbled her way to the 1976 Olympics as an assistant coach. In 1982, she was named the head coach of the LSU women's basketball team.

She won 422 games in 22 seasons at LSU before her health forced her to step down. She was inducted into the Naismith Basketball Hall of Fame in 2005.

From little Walnut Grove, Sue Gunter hit the big time.

Did you know there's a town in Louisiana named Pigeon? And a place called Beaver? There's even one named Roy. And another village called Lucky.

They're little places, not on an interstate highway. They're off major highways, pretty much in the middle of nowhere.

But don't get those towns wrong. They are special and wonderful. That's because God is in Weyanoke and in Effie, just like he is in Baton Rouge, Shreveport, and Monroe.

As Jacob found out one morning, the middle of nowhere is holy ground — because God is there.

Get a Louisiana map and find some funny names of towns. Remind yourself that God is in each one of them.

GOOD-BYE

Read John 13:33-36.

Jesus told Peter, "Where I am going, you can't follow now."

LSU once threw a good-bye party, but the honoree wouldn't go away.

On May 11, 2008, LSU whipped Miss. State 9-6 in the last game scheduled at old Alex Box Stadium. The 70-year-old ballpark was to give way to a new stadium already being built.

Fans took a lot of pictures. More than 100 former players took a victory lap. They were all there to say good-bye to an old friend.

The athletic director peeled the last piece off a stadium countdown sign. It now read "0 Games Remaining at the Box."

It was a lovely good-bye party. But maybe it wasn't really good-bye. The AD's wife thought so. Over the countdown zero sign, she put one that said "NCAA Still to Come!"

Tigers

Sure enough, the stadium hosted an NCAA regional. Then it would be good-bye, right? Nope. LSU won it and The Box hosted a super regional. Only when LSU won that, too, and was on the way to the College World Series did the stadium finally say good-bye.

Even though you're a youngster, you have probably known good-byes — and they hurt. Maybe your best friend moved away. Maybe you moved away and had to tell a whole lot of your friends and buddies good-bye. It's sad to stand and wave while your grandparents drive off on their way home after a visit.

Jesus knows just how you feel. He always had his friends around him, but it came time for him to tell them good-bye. He was going away; he would leave them.

But Jesus wasn't just moving to another town. He was about to finish his mission on Earth. He would provide a way so that none of us would ever have to say good-bye again.

List some people you have said good-bye to. Get their addresses from a parent and write them a note.

PLAN AHEAD

Read Psalm 33:4-11.

The plans of the Lord stand firm forever.

Getting a football team to and from a bowl game takes a lot of planning. One time, however, the Tigers got caught with no way to get home.

LSU hit the road to Miami after receiving an Orange Bowl bid in 1943. The Tigers pulled off an upset, beating Texas A&M 19-14.

So far, everything had gone according to plan. But then came a glitch. This was the middle of World War II. With soldiers being moved across the country, berths on a train weren't available for the Tigers. Neither were seats on a commercial flight.

So a former LSU student manager came up with a plan that bailed the team out. He was now a banker who owned a car dealership in

Baton Rouge. He got in touch with a fellow car dealer in Miami he had done business with and bought a whole bunch of used cars.

The team drove home in the cars. The car dealer/banker then put them on his car lot and sold them. Head coach Bernie Moore, by the way, got the best car: a Cadillac.

People make plans every single day. You do, too. You plan to go to school. You plan to do your chores. You plan to go spend some time with your grandparents.

But what if something happens to mess up your plans? What if you wake up sick so you can't go swimming or play baseball like you planned? Sometimes even when you make a great plan, it doesn't work out, does it?

God has plans for you, too. God's plan for you has nothing but good things like happiness, love, and kindness. But it will work only if you make God the boss of your life.

What are your plans for tomorrow? Tomorrow night, think back and see if they turned out the way you planned.

WHO, ME?

Read Judges 6:12-16.

"Lord," Gideon asked, "how can I save Israel? I'm a nobody even in my own family."

Coach Nick Saban gave Rohan Davey the surprise of his life. An LSU win in the 2000 Peach Bowl was the result.

"I wasn't even thinking I might be going in," Davey said at halftime. He was the "almost-forgotten backup." He hadn't taken a single snap at quarterback in the last five games.

But the Tigers trailed Ga. Tech 14-3, and the offense hadn't done much of anything. So Saban turned to Davey and surprised him.

"It was like turning on a light switch," said safety Ryan Clark. In the last half, Davey went 17 for 25 passing and threw three touchdowns. The Davey-led Tigers outscored Tech 25-0 in the last half and won 28-14.

Tigers

Why was the surprising move made in the first place? "What we needed was an emotional lift," said one LSU assistant coach. "Ro was our emotional leader."

The backup who was surprised he got to play was surprised again after the season. The players voted him a permanent team captain.

You ever said, "Who, me?" as Rohan Davey did. Maybe when the teacher called on you in class? Or when somebody asked you to sing a solo? Your stomach kind of knots up, doesn't it? You get real nervous, too.

That's the way Gideon felt when God called on him to lead his people in battle. And you might feel the same way when somebody calls on you to say a prayer. Or to read a part in Sunday school.

Hey, I can't do that, you might say. But you can. God wants you to do stuff for him. Like Gideon, God thinks you can do it just fine. And with God's help, you will. Just like Gideon.

Think of some ways you can help at Sunday school. And then volunteer.

DAY 59

HEAD GAMES

Read Job 28:20-28.

*Respect God, which will show that
you are wise.*

LSU head coach Bernie Moore thought about
football every chance he got. Most folks just
thought he was absentminded.

From 1935-47, Moore won 83 games. He
also coached track and won a national title.
LSU's outdoor track facility is named for him.

Each day Moore would drive to a drug store
across from the campus to get some coffee.
There, he would start thinking about football
plays. He would be thinking so hard that often
he got lost on his way back to his office.

One time Moore asked a student to write a
letter for him. He started talking and the student started writing. The coach stopped and
looked out a window, thinking about football.

After a few minutes, he turned around, saw

the student, and asked, "Good morning, son. What can I do for you?"

During games, he paced all the time. He would often stop, pluck a blade of grass, and stick it between his teeth without knowing he was doing it. He never swallowed It.

Have you noticed that you use your brain all the time every day (like Bernie Moore and football)? In every class at school, you have to use your brain so you'll be smarter.

The same thing applies to your faith in God and Jesus. When you go to church or open your Bible, you need to keep on thinking. You seek Jesus with all you have: with your heart, your soul, your body, and your mind.

There's nothing strange about using your brain to think about God. That's because God gave you your brain to begin with. That means he likes people to be smart.

So for God, loving him and trusting in Jesus is the smartest thing of all.

Open your Bible at random and read a few verses. Use your brain to figure out what they mean as best you can.

DAY 60

UNEXPECTEDLY

Read Luke 2:1-7.

Mary gave birth to her first child. It was a boy she named Jesus.

The experts knew what to expect in the 2001 SEC Championship Game. LSU just didn't give them what they expected.

Tennessee was 10-1 and ranked No. 2. They would play for the national title with a win. LSU meanwhile had "sneaked" into the SEC title game with a 5-3 conference record and some good tiebreakers.

It got worse when LSU's starting quarterback and starting tailback got injured. Matt Mauck and Domanick Davis unexpectedly stepped up to lead the Tigers to a 24-17 lead early in the fourth quarter.

UT got a first down at the LSU 4-yard line, and something unexpected happened again. Freshman cornerback Travis Daniels had not played a down all season. He went in for an injured player, and UT threw his way. He broke up the pass. The Vols kicked a field goal, and unexpectedly they were done. LSU won 31-20.

Something is unexpected when you didn't know it was going to happen. It can be good or bad. Maybe your school was supposed to have a field day but thunder, lightning, and rain wiped that out. Or you found a dollar bill on the sidewalk. Life surprises us a lot.

God is just like that. He surprises us so we can remember that he's still around. Like the time he was born as the baby Jesus.

There is nothing that God can't do in your life. The only thing that holds God back is when you don't believe he can do something. Or when you don't live each day with God in your heart and on your mind.

You should always be ready for God to do something unexpected in your life.

Tell about a time you expected one thing and got something completely different. Was it a good or a bad surprise?

DAY 61

COMEBACK KIDS

Read Acts 9:18-22.

Those who heard Paul asked, "Isn't he the one who persecuted and killed Christians in Jerusalem?"

Behind 13-0. Offense doing nothing. That's where the Tigers were at halftime of the 1968 Sugar Bowl. Then they pulled a comeback.

LSU had only one first down and 38 total yards in a miserable first half against sixth-ranked Wyoming. But LSU head coach Charles McClendon made some changes at the break.

For one thing, he put a bunch of reserves into the game. The offense drove 80 yards for a touchdown right off the bat. Tailback Glenn Smith, the game's MVP, scored from the one.

The defense forced a punt, and the Tigers roared into the end zone again. Quarterback Nelson Stokley hit end Tommy Morel with an 8-yard TD pass. The comeback stalled when the extra point was no good, leaving the score tied at 13.

But the Tigers were rolling, and they scored again with only 4:32 on the clock. That locked up the comeback and the 20-13 upset win.

A comeback means you come from behind. You know by now that you don't always win. You make an A on a test one day and sprain your ankle the next. You do all your chores at home but get in trouble for talking in class.

In life, even for a kid, winning isn't about never losing. Things will go wrong for you sometimes. Winning means you pick yourself up from your defeat and keep going. You make a comeback of your own, just like Paul did and the Tigers did against unbeaten Wyoming.

Besides, God's grace is always there for you, so your comeback can always be bigger than your setback. With Jesus in your life, it's not how you start that counts; it's how you finish.

Remember a time a team you like made a comeback. Compare that to a time you came back when something went wrong.

DAY 62

STAR POWER

Read Luke 10:1-3, 17-20.

The Lord appointed 72 others and sent them out two by two.

To have a chance at the SEC title and the national championship, LSU had to defeat a team with a true star.

The Tigers were 9-1 and ranked third on Nov. 22, 2003, when they went to Oxford to play Ole Miss. The Rebels were led by their star quarterback, Eli Manning. It would be the Rebel star against the Tiger defense.

The defense won as the game was low scoring. LSU led 10-7 at halftime.

On the first play of the last quarter, Tiger quarterback Matt Mauck and receiver Devery Henderson teamed up for a 53-yard touchdown pass. LSU led 17-7.

Manning finally got something going, but it wasn't enough against the Tiger defense. The

Tigers

Rebels had three late chances to win or tie the game, but the star couldn't beat the defense.

The Tigers won a tough one 17-14 and went on to win the national title.

Football teams and other groups may have a star. They wouldn't be much of anything, though, without everybody else to help out. How far can a running back go without his line up front to block for him?

It's the same way with the team known as the church. Your church has a star. It's the pastor or preacher, who is a trained pro, the leader, the one up front on Sunday.

But Jesus didn't have any stars to help him. He just had a bunch of no-names who loved him. Nothing has changed. The church has its star. What it needs is people who aren't stars, people who do whatever they can for the sake of God's kingdom because they love Jesus.

God's church needs you.

What's your pastor's name? If he's the star, name some folks in your church who aren't stars. Tell what they do.

FEAR FACTOR

Read Matthew 14:25-31.

Jesus said, "Be brave. It is I. Don't be afraid."

One day at baseball practice, Greg Smith was suddenly afraid.

During the fall of 2002, Smith, a freshman pitcher, was running the bases as he had so many times before. His heart started beating very fast.

"I waited for it to slow down," he said, but it didn't. He made it home to his apartment. "If I lifted up my shirt, you could actually see my chest moving, beating real fast."

After several hours, his heart finally slowed, but Smith was exhausted. "I couldn't even get up to take a shower I was so tired," he said.

He knew what had happened wasn't normal. He saw a doctor and learned he did indeed have a heart condition. That scared Smith and his family even more.

But it wasn't life-threatening. He underwent a pair of procedures and was back on the field for the 2003 season. He got tired faster when he ran, but he could still pitch. He was first-team All-SEC in 2005, got drafted, and wound up in the major leagues in 2008.

Most everybody's afraid of snakes and big old hairy spiders. Lots of folks don't like bad weather very much. Or high places.

Over and over in the Bible Jesus tells us not to be afraid. Does this mean not to fear a car that's coming at you? How about a big, slobbery dog that doesn't look too friendly?

Of course not. Fear is a helpful thing God put in you to help keep you safe.

What Jesus is talking about is being afraid of everything. Living in fear all the time. God says don't live like that. Trust in him, be brave, and he will calm your fears.

Think of two things you're afraid of. Are they things you should be afraid of or are they silly fears? Ask God to help you lose the fear of silly stuff.

DAY 64

STRANGE BUT TRUE

Read Philippians 2:5-11.

Jesus is God, but he became a servant and died on a cross.

Talk about a strange game! It wasn't played in the United States, and part of the game plan was to make an opponent barf.

On Christmas Day of 1907, LSU became the first American football team to play a game outside the country. The Tigers went down to Cuba and took on the University of Havana.

LSU's coach was most worried about all the good food the friendly folks fed his players. The favorite was stewed chicken and rice.

During their warm-ups, the Tigers noticed some drinking glasses, each filled with wine, on the Cuban bench. The Cuban players would run over and take big swigs of the wine.

George "Doc" Fenton noticed a 300-pound Cuban player drinking a whole lot of the wine.

He told a teammate, "Hit that guy in the stomach with your head and he's done for."

Right off the bat, a Tiger lineman fired right into the Cuban's stomach. Fenton said, "The big guy sprouted like a well. We nearly had to swim out of there."

The Tigers won the strange game 56-0.

A lot of things about life are strange. Isn't it strange that you can't eat all the sugar you want to? Isn't it strange that you can't play all the time when everybody knows that's what kids are good at?

God's kind of strange, too, isn't he? He's the ruler of all the universe; he can do anything he wants to. And so he let himself be killed by a bunch of men who nailed him to two pieces of wood. Isn't that downright weird?

And why did God do it? That's strange, too. He did it because he loves you so much. In the person of Jesus, God died so that you can be a part of his family.

List five things about God that are strange. Tell why they're strange.

WATER POWER

Read Acts 10:44-48.

Peter asked, "Can anyone keep these people from being baptized with water?"

Did the Tigers use water one time to pull off a dirty trick that helped them win a game?

It looked suspicious. It hadn't rained for a long time. Still, the Tiger Stadium turf was as wet as it could be for the game against North Carolina in 1949. The angry UNC coaches said LSU had wet the field to slow down their great running back, Charlie "Choo Choo" Justice.

LSU head coach Gaynell Tinsley knew he hadn't told anyone to soak the field. So he turned detective to find out what happened.

The groundskeeper always watered the field the night before a game. But Tinsley wanted the Tigers to work out, so he told the groundskeeper not to worry about it.

After the workout, along came the student manager, who saw that the field hadn't been watered. So he did it. Then the groundskeeper thought the field hadn't been watered, so he turned the hoses on the next morning.

It wasn't a dirty trick, and all the water may not have helped. Still, LSU upset UNC 13-7. At the time, it was LSU's greatest win ever.

Do you like to go swimming? Or take a boat ride? Man, the beach is cool with all that sand and sun and those waves. Is anything more fun and exciting than a big old water slide?

Water is fun, but it's a lot more than that. You need it to stay alive. You have to drink water every day.

Water is so important that it is even a part of your faith in Jesus. It's called baptism. A person who is baptized — including you — is marked by the water as someone who belongs to Jesus. It tells the world you are a Christian and that Jesus is your Lord.

Have you been baptized? If so, talk about what it was like. If not, is it time?

NAME IT

Read Exodus 3:13-15.

Moses asked God what his name was. God answered, "Tell them I AM has sent you."

One LSU star's unusual name won him an online poll.

He was defensive end Barkevious Mingo. He was twice second-team All-SEC (2011 and '12) and turned pro in 2013.

He won that online poll in 2010 as word of his rather strange name spread. He beat out the likes of Iris Macadangang and Taco Vandervelde, both real people.

Mingo's unusual name was his mama's idea. Barbara Johnson started with the first part of her name and added the tail end of cousin Alkevious's name. His dad went along with it.

Mingo said his mother had to work with him "every day to make sure I spelled my name right." People still had trouble saying it right: "bar-KEE-vee-us." When Barkevious arrived at LSU in 2010, folks greeted him with cellphone pictures of dogs they'd named after him.

Your name is not just a label to keep people from hollering, "Hey, you" at you all the time. When your friends and classmates hear your name, they think of something about you.

This is really true in the Bible. The names of people in the Bible told other people something about them. Maybe how they acted. Or if they were strong or godly people.

The same is true of the name of God. At Mt. Horeb, God told Moses what his name was: Yahweh or "I Am." God told us his name as another way to let us get close to him. You have to know someone's name to be a friend.

As for you, what do you think your name says about you to God? Remember this: Just as you know God's name, he knows yours, too.

Have an adult help you look up the meaning of your first name. Does it match who you are and what you're like?

DAY 67

PRAYER WARRIORS

Read Luke 18:1-5.

Jesus told his disciples a story to show them they should always pray and never give up.

The loss was so sudden and so shocking that LSU's athletic director could only pray.

"Lord, what do we do now? Please guide my decision. It is in your hands now." That was the prayer of Paul Dietzel in January of 1980.

The athletic director spent more than a year searching for a new head football coach. He hired Bo Rein. Only 34 years old, Rein was the head man at North Carolina State.

On Jan. 9, 1980, Rein and his pilot were flying home from a recruiting trip. Something went wrong. The plane veered off course and couldn't be reached by radio. Later, more than 1,000 miles off course, it crashed into the Atlantic Ocean. Rein had been LSU's head coach for 42 days.

That's when Dietzel turned to prayer for God's help. He got it when Jerry Stovall, a two-time LSU All-American back, stepped up to lead the program out of its darkest hour.

Jesus told us that   like Paul Dietzel — we should always pray and never give up. But what do you think is the right way to pray? Do you have to get on your knees? Can you be by yourself, or do you have to be in church? Should you pray out loud or can you whisper?

The truth is there is no right or wrong way to pray. What counts is that you pray, and that you mean it from your heart. Here's another truth: God hears every one of your prayers.

Sometimes — and we don't know why — God doesn't answer prayers right away. And sometimes God's answer is "no" because he always knows what's best for you even when you don't.

But no matter what, you keep praying.

Talk about the last time God answered one of your prayers.

THAT HURTS!

Read 2 Corinthians 1:3-7.

*God is the father of all comfort in
our pain and our suffering.*

Tommy Hodson kept playing in a game even after he had bitten his tongue almost in two!

Hodson is the only LSU player ever to be named first-team All-SEC four times. He quarterbacked the Tigers to two SEC titles.

In the Kentucky game of 1986, he was hit hard after he threw a pass. That's when he bit right through his tongue.

A local dentist led him to the dressing room. "You bit all the way through it," he told Hodson. The dentist had to put three stitches on the top and two more on the bottom to hold the quarterback's tongue together.

Hodson hurt so bad he figured he wouldn't play anymore that day. He was wrong because the LSU coach put him back in. He threw two touchdown passes and LSU won 25-16.

Hodson wound up with a scar on his chin. Some folks think the story isn't true, but it is. Hodson played after not just biting his tongue, but biting through It. That had to hurt.

Does a day go by when you don't feel pain? A scrape from a fall. A blister from your shoes. A goose egg on your head. A bruise from a football or soccer game.

Some pain isn't just on your body. It's a different kind of hurt when someone calls you names or makes fun of you and embarrasses you. It still hurts an awful lot, though.

Jesus knows all about pain. After all, they drove nails into his hands and feet, hung him on two pieces of wood, and stuck a spear in his side. It was an awful, painful way to die.

So when you hurt, you can find comfort in Jesus. He's been there before. He knows all about tears and pain.

Look over your body for bumps, bruises, scratches, and scrapes. Tell how you got each one and how bad it hurt.

NERVOUS NELLIE

Read Mark 5:1-13.

The demon begged, "Jesus, promise you won't hurt me!"

Kicker Trent Domingue was so nervous his whole body was shaking. But he still scored the game-winning touchdown.

LSU and Florida met in 2015 in a showdown of undefeated teams. The score was tied at 28 in the fourth quarter.

With less than eleven minutes to play, the Tigers lined up for a 33-yard field goal. It was a gimme for Domingue, a junior who hadn't missed a field goal all season. But head coach Les Miles called for a fake.

The holder took the snap and tossed an overhead pass to Dominigue. He promptly bobbled it. "How many bobbles were there?" Miles asked. "My heart fluttered with every bobble."

With the ball finally under control, Domingue

took off and scored. LSU won 35-28.

"I was pretty nervous," he said. "My whole body was shaking." He was so nervous he forgot he still had to kick the extra point.

Like Trent Domingue, you get nervous sometimes. Before a big test maybe. Or before a big game. How about having to make a speech? Whoowee, that's tough.

Have you ever thought that you make other people nervous? That there's one for sure who really gets nervous about you? Who in the world? Believe it or not, it's Satan himself. Yep, that's the one.

As a Christian, you make Satan nervous because you stand before him with the power of Jesus Christ to use. When you live for Jesus, you spend the day making the devil himself downright miserable.

So go out there and have a good time making Satan nervous. Do everything in Jesus' name.

At a mirror, say the name of Jesus
out loud and act out how a nervous,
scared devil might react.

FUN HOUSE

Read Nehemiah 8:1-3, 9-12.

The people ate and drank and celebrated with great joy.

Are you having fun?" Since a national title was on the line, it was an interesting time for a coach to ask that question.

The coach was Chuck Winstead, head of the LSU men's golf team. The player he asked about having fun was senior All-American Ben Taylor. The place was the next-to-last hole of the 2015 national championship tournament.

Taylor trailed by one stroke. If he could win the last two holes, the Tigers would be the national champs. As Taylor got ready to hit his second shot, his coach asked his question. "It was hard to say no because it was a lot of fun," Taylor said later.

It wound up a whole lot of fun. Relaxed by the surprising question, Taylor did indeed win the last two holes. He sank an 8-foot par putt on 18, and the Tigers were national champs!

The fun really began then. Taylor dropped his putter as his excited teammates raced up the fairway and joined him for a group hug.

A lot of people think that Christians should always be out trying to keep folks from having fun. But that is so, so wrong.

The Israelites cried when Ezra read them God's law because they had failed God. But Nehemiah told them not to cry, to go throw a party instead! Go eat some burgers and drink some sodas with your buddies, he said. That shows you right there how God feels about having fun. He's for it.

It should be that way for you. Having fun is a form of celebrating all that God has given you, which is everything you have. Especially your salvation in Jesus.

To live for Jesus is to know the fun in living.

***Do something that is so much fun
it makes you laugh. Remember
that's how God wants you to live.***

NOTES

(by devotion number)

1   was surprised to find . . . cleats on leather shoes.: Marty Mule, *Eye of the Tiger* (Atlanta: Longstreet Press, 1993), pp. 1-2.

1   Word got around town . . . team chose a ref,: Dan Hardesty, *The Louisiana Tigers* (Huntsville, AL: The Strode Publishers, 1975) pp. 15, 16, 18.

2   The Wildcat coach . . . juggled it,: Marty Mule, *Game of My Life* (Champaign, IL: Sports Publishing L.L.C., 2006), pp. 91, 93.

2   "It was like a . . . couldn't believe it.": Mule, *Game of My Life*, p. 96.

3   He held for extra . . . so he could play.: Austin Murphy, "The 2007 BCS Championship," *Sports Illustrated Presents LSU Tigers: 2007 National Champions*, Jan 16, 2008, p. 39.

3   It's been tough, but right now it's so, so sweet.": Murphy, "The 2007 BCS Championship," p. 44.

4   Before the 2015 game, . . . pretty mad about it,": David Ching, "LSU's Leonard Fournette Makes Auburn Pay," *ESPN.com*, Sept. 20, 2015, http://espn.go.com/blog/sec/post/_id/106847.

4   "humiliating Auburn defenders.": David Ching, "LSU's Leonard Fournette."

4   "It was fun," . . . some great football,": Ross Dellenger, "Behind Leonard Fournette's 228 Rushing Yards," *The Advocate*, Sept. 19, 2015, http://theadvocate.com/sports/lsu/13490566128.

6   "the longest one-mile move in history.": David Helman, "Softball: Current, Former Tigers Excited," *Daily Reveille*, Feb. 16, 2009, http://www.lsureveille.com/softball.

6   Since, 2004, the softball . . . place, but she didn't.: Helman, "Softball."

6   "We have no . . . fans to park.": Matt DeVille, "Girouard, LSU Ready," *TigerRag.com*, Feb. 11, 2009, http://www.tigerrag.com?p=6661.

7   The 1972 football . . . Tiger Stadium history.: Hardesty, pp. 289-90.

7   "Bert, this is what you came to LSU for.": Mule, *Game of My Life*, p. 119.

7   After the game, . . . winked at me!" Mule, *Game of My Life*, p. 173.

8   DiNardo decided to . . . all game long.: Mule, *Game of My Life*, p. 237.

9   They were backed up . . . down the left sideline.: Hardesty, p. 116.

10   After the game, . . . didn't say anything.: Mule, *Game of My Life*, p. 4.

10   Again, the head . . . things would get better.: Mule, *Game of My Life*, p. 4.

11   He hurt so bad . . . tie his shoes.: Lee Feinswog, *Tales from the LSU Sidelines* (Champaign, IL: Sports Publishing L.L.C., 2002), p. 11.

11   "It was killing . . . it never did.": Feinswog, *Tales from the LSU Sidelines*.

12   At a U.S. . . . after the show.: Bruce Hunter and Joe Planas, *Fighting Tigers Basketball* (Chicago: Bonus Books, Inc., 1991), pp, 25-26.

12   The kid stood . . . "Your dad around?": Curry Kirkpatrick, "Shack Attack," *Sports Illustrated*, Jan. 21, 1991, http://sportsillustrated.cnn.com/vault/article/magazine/MAG1118770/index.htm.

12   When Shaq's family . . . from Coach Brown,": Hunter and Planas, p. 26.

13   The third team . . . on the Bandits. Mule, *Game of My Life*, pp.135-38.

14   It happened way back . . . without winning at 6-0.: Hardesty, pp. 24-25.

15   The school changed . . . more than once.: Mule, Game of My Life, p. 135.

16   "It's the earliest . . . or some shade.: Carl Dubois, "LSU Opener Anything But Normal," *The Advocate*, Aug. 31, 2008, http://docs.newsbank.com/w/InfoWeb/aggdocs/Newsbank.

17   Before the game, all . . . what was coming.: Cory McCartney, "One Title Down," *Sports Illustrated Presents LSU Tigers*, Jan. 16, 2008, p. 35.

18   His goal growing up . . . wanted him to be.: "Shoot out the Moon," *LSU Campus*, http://www.lsu.edu/highlights/051/maravich.html.

19   "an incredible, absolutely unbelievable run to glory.": Hardesty, p. 211.

20   At a night game . . . just seen, it's heard!: John Logue quoted in *SEC Sports Quotes*, Ed. Chris Warner (Baton Rouge: CEW Enterprises, 2002), p. 160.

20   "The Golden Band . . . uses the sousaphones.: Frank B. Wickes, "LSU Band History," *LSU Department of Bands*, http://www.bands.lsu.edu/band_history/index.php.

21   Davis walked off the . . . since the seventh grade.: Randy Rosetta, "Big Makeover," *The Advocate*, July 30, 2006, http://docs.newsbank.com/s/InfoWeb/aggdocs/NewsBank.

22   In the fall of 2001, . . . back on my head.": Scott Rabalais, "LSU's Robinson Enjoys Practice," *The Advocate*, March 26, 2002. http://docs.newsbank.com/s/InfoWeb/aggdocs/NewsBank.

23   Short on cash, some . . . the Tigers and won big.: Hardesty, p. 52.

23   In 1992, fans got to the . . . who walked into town.: Hardesty, p. 56.

24   He taught himself by . . . his yard at home. Mule, *Game of My Life*, p. 178.

24   "I needed it," . . . to catch my breath.": Mule, *Game of My Life*, p. 178.

25   When he was 10, . . . when he was 13,: Randy Rosetta, "Giving Back," *The Advocate*, July 18, 2008, http://docs.newsbank.com/s/InfoWeb/aggdocs/NewsBank.

25   never got to go . . . "Couldn't afford it,": Tim MacMahon, "Brandon Bass' Camp," *Dallas Mavericks Blog*, June 21, 2008, http://mavsblog.dallasnews.com/archives/2008/06.

25   "God has blessed . . . give something back.": Rosetta, "Giving Back."

26   Late in the one-sided . . . the happy students.: Bernell Ballard, "Tigers Stun Ole Miss," *Greatest Moments in LSU Football History*, Francis J. Fitzgerald, ed. (Champaign, IL: Sports Publishing L.L.C., 2002), p. 89.

26   "the most important victory of my life.": Ballard, p. 89.

27   The stands weren't finished . . . the rest of the way.: Hardesty, pp. 62-64.

28   Sugar Bowl officials were in . . . agreed to the bowl game.: Hardesty, pp. 164-65.

29   All through the tournament, . . . took a victory lap.: Brian Hendrickson, "LSU Fans Prove to Be Class Act," *Wilmington Star-News*, June 2, 2003, reprinted in *The Advocate*, June 22, 2003, http://docs.newsbank.com/s/InfoWeb/aggdocs/NewsBank.

30   World War II cut into . . . the students gave in.: Feinswog, pp. 102-03.

31   The first game was . . . "only defeated once.": Hunter and Planas, pp. 115-16.

32   "there were lots of . . . football a little longer.: Mule, *Game of My Life*, p. 219.

33   The football seasons way . . . enough time to practice.: Hardesty, pp. 26-27.

34   LSU played what a sportswriter said was a perfect game.: Hardesty, p. 253.

34   "The Tigers were hopelessly outmatched,": Hardesty, p. 250.

34   "We didn't make a mistake,": Hardesty, p. 253.

35   Basketball is the silliest . . . who can beat me?": Hunter and Planas, p. 89.

35   He showed up in . . . in an old [handkerchief.": Hunter and Planas, p. 84.

35   He worked himself into . . . to his teammates.: Hunter and Planas, pp. 83-84.

36   The fans made so . . . up on the seismograph. Kristine Calongne, "After 15 Years, Auburn-LSU Game Still an Earthshaking Experience," *LSU Campus: LSU Highlights Winter 2003*, http://www.lsu.edu/highlights/033/football.html.

37   The Tigers made their . . . in World War II.: Hardesty, pp. 138-39.

38   "nearly 4$^{1/2}$ hours of . . . long as it takes.": Scott Rabalais, "LSU Stays Alive,"

The Advocate, May 21, 2000, http://docs.newsbank.com/s/InfoWeb/
    aggdocs/NewsBank.

39   When Hilliard showed up . . . anyone we have.": Mule, Eye of the Tiger, p. 195.

40   Davis "looked like a . . . his go-to receiver.: Mule, Game of My Life, pp. 64, 66.

41   The fans didn't like . . . assistant coach from Texas.: Hardesty, pp. 49-50.

42   His first day on . . . take any plays off.": Randy Rosetta, "Happy to Be There,"
        The Advocate, Sept. 10, 2008, http://docs.newsbank.com/s/InfoWeb/agg
        docs/NewsBank.

43   Dietzel made sure every . . . watch three minutes fast.: Feinswog, pp. 58-59.

44   LSU quarterback Y.A. . . . the Hall of Fame.: Mule, Eye of the Tiger, p. 103.

44   Against Ole Miss in . . . I could have scored,": Mule, Eye of the Tiger, pp. 103-04.

45   Oklahoma even offered for . . . before the game!: Tiger Terrific! (Chicago:
        Triumph Books, 2004), p. 10.

46   "the freak show of . . . the motor burned up.: Kent Lowe, Sr., "Look Back: 20
        Years After LSU, Loyola Marymount," LSUsports.net, Feb. 3, 2010, http://
        www.lsusports.net/ViewArticle.dbml.

47   Louisiana Gov. Huey . . . pro, not an amateur.: Mule, Eye of the Tiger, pp. 43-44.

48   "We wanted to win . . . a recipe for grits!: Kelli Anderson, "Home Is Where the
        Heart Is," Sports Illustrated, Sept. 19, 2005, http://vault.sportsillustrated.
        cnn.com/vault/article/magazine/MAG1106374/index.htm.

49   Early on, he hurt . . . bone in his hand. "Warren Morris," TheGoal.com, http://
        www.thegoal.com/players/baseball/warren_morris/morris21_warren.html.

50   LSU's first mascot was . . . on their jackets.: Mule, Eye of the Tiger, p. 5.

50   that year, the team . . . Yankee body parts!: Mule, Eye of the Tiger, pp. 6-7.

50   The first live cat was . . . afraid of all the noise.: Feinswog, p. 95.

50   In 1936, a student named . . . came up with the idea.: Feinswog, p. 98.

51   "a feeble-looking, yet . . . since the 1960s.: Jimmy Hyams, "Risher & Tigers Upset
        Alabama, 20-10," The Greatest Moments in LSU Football History, Francis J.
        Fitzgerald, ed., pp. 113-14.

52   "a great model of a Christian gentleman.": Hunter and Planas, p. 108.

52   "the most pure Christian . . . to meet in life. Hunter and Planas, pp. 103-04.

52   a man who never . . . after the departing bus.: Hunter and Planas, p. 108.

53   Exactly why it started . . . sat in the rain.: "LSU Football Traditions A to Z," 2009
        LSU Football Media Guide, p.63, http://www.lsusports.net/ViewArticle.dbml.

53   "the freakiest, funkiest . . . all of college football.: Matt Hayes, Sporting News
        Today, quoted in "Saturday Night in Death Valley," p. 34.

54   he played with a . . . while his friends played.: Cory McCartney, "A Tiger
        Unchained," Sports Illustrated Presents LSU Tigers: 2007 National
        Champions, Jan. 16, 2008, pp. 47-49.

54   He took a football . . . dreamed of playing.: John K. Davis, "Glenn Dorsey,"
        suite101.com, Jan. 5, 2008, http://college-football.suite101.com/article.com.

54   By age 8, his . . . for him to play.: McCartney, "A Tiger Unchained," p. 48.

55   That's where Gunter grew . . . learn to dribble.": "For Gunter, 40th Season as
        Good as the First," LSU Campus: LSU Highlights Spring 2004, http://www.
        lsu.edu/highlights/041/gunter.html.

56   Fans took a lot . . . Still to Come!": Carl Dubois, "Tigers Hoping for One More Lap,"
        The Advocate, May 12, 2008, http://docs.newsbank.com/s/InfoWeb/agg
        docs/NewsBank.

57   berths on a train . . . the best car: a Cadillac.: Hardestry, pp. 147-48.

58   "I wasn't even thinking . . . on a light switch,": Mule, Game of My Life, pp. 50-51.

58   "What we needed was . . . our emotional leader.": Mule, Game of My Life, p. 53.

59   Each day Moore would . . . He never swallowed it.: Hardesty, p. 112.

60   had "sneaked into . . . some good tiebreakers.: Feinswog, p. 14.

60   Freshman cornerback Travis . . . an injured player,: Feinswog, p. 15.

63   During the fall of . . . he could still pitch.: Carl Dubois, "Learning to Slow Down," *The Advocate*, June 1, 2005, http://docs.newsbank.com/s/InfoWeb/agg docs/NewsBank.

64   On Christmas Day of . . . swim out of there.": Mule, *Eye of the Tiger*, pp. 26-28.

65   It hadn't rained for . . . on the next morning.: Hardesty, p. 162.

66   He won that online . . . they'd named after him.: Andrew Lawrence, "And Mingo Was His Name," *Sports Illustrated*, April 15, 2013, http://sportsillustrated. cnn.com/vault/article/magazine/MAG1207388/index.htm.

67   "Lord, what do we . . . coach for 42 days.: Marvin West, "In a Difficult Hour, The Torch Is Passed," *The Greatest Moments in LSU Football History*, Francis J. Fitzgerald, ed (Champaign, ILi Sports Publishing L.L.C., /011/), p. 118

68   In the Kentucky game . . . coach put him back in.: Feinswog, pp. 4-5.

69   "How many bobbles were . . . with every bobble.": Ross Dellenger, "Trick-Play Touchdown Lifts No. 6 LSU," *The Advocate*, Oct. 27, 2015, http://the advocate.com/sports/lsu/13732448-171/trick-play-touchdown-lifts-no-6.

69   "I was pretty nervous," he said. "My whole body was shaking.": "Fake Field Goal, Leonard Fournette's 2 TDs Carry LSU over Florida," *ESPN.go.com*, Oct. 28, 2015, http://espn.go.com/ncf/recap?gameId=400603893.

69   he forgot he still had to kick the extra point.: Dellenger, "Trick-Play Touchdown."

70   Are you having fun?": Will Stafford, "NATIONAL CHAMPIONS! Men's Golf Beats USC 4-1," *LSUsports.net*, June 4, 2015. http://www.lsusports.net/View Article.dbml?ATCLID=210127490.

70   "It was hard to say no because it was a lot of fun,": Will Stafford, "NATIONAL CHAMPIONS!"

70   Taylor dropped his putter . . . for a group hug.: "LSU Claims 5th NCAA Golf Title to End 60-Year Drought," *ESPN.go.com*, June 3, 2015, http://espn.go.com/ college-sports/story/_/id/1300672/lsu-claims-th-ncaa-golf-title-end-60-year-drought.

WORKS USED

Ballard, Bernell. "Tigers Stun Ole Miss, Orange Bowl Brass." *Greatest Moments in LSU Football History.* Francis J. Fitzgerald, ed. Champaign, IL: Sports Publishing L.L.C., 2002. 89.

Calongne, Kristine. "After 15 Years, LSU-Auburn Game Still an Earthshaking Experience." *LSU Campus: LSU Highlights Winter 2003.* http://www.lsu.edu/highlights/033/football.html.

Ching, David. "LSU's Leonard Fournette Makes Auburn Pay for Midweek Trash Talk. *ESPN.com.* 20 Sept. 2015. http://espn.go.com/blog/sec/post/_/id/106847.

Davis, John K. "Glenn Dorsey: Key to LSU Defense." *suite101.com.* 5 Jan. 2008, http://college-football.suite101.com/article/cfm/glenn_dorsey_key_to_lsu_defense.

Dellenger, Ross. "Behind Leonard Fournette's 228 Rushing Yards, LSU Crushes Auburn 45-21." *The Advocate.* 19 Sept. 2015. http://theadvocate.com/sports/lsu/13490566128.

-----. "Trick-Play Touchdown Lifts No. 6 LSU to 35-28 Victory over No. 8 Florida." *The Advocate.* 17 Oct. 2015. http://theadvocate.com/sports/lsu/13732448-171/trick-play-touchdown-lifts-no-6.

DeVille, Matt. "Girouard, LSU Ready to Take the Field at New Tiger Park," *TigerRag.com.* 11 Feb. 2009. http://www.tigerrag.com?p=6661.

Dubois, Carl. "Learning to Slow Down: LSU Left-Hander Smith Overcoming Condition That Causes Rapid Heartbeat." *The Advocate.* 1 June 2005. http://docs.newsbank.com/s/InfoWeb/aggdocs/NewsBank.

-----. "LSU Opener Anything But Normal." *The Advocate.* 31 Aug. 2008. http://docs.newsbank.com/s/InfoWeb/aggdocs/NewsBank.

-----. "Tigers Hoping for One More Lap at The Box." *The Advocate.* 12 May 2008. http://docs.newsbank.com/s/InfoWeb/aggdocs/NewsBank.

"Fake Field Goal, Leonard Fournette's Two TDs Carry LSU over Florida." *ESPN. go.com.* 18 Oct. 2015. http://espn.go.com/ncf/recap?gameId=400603893.

Feinswog, Lee. *Tales from the LSU Sidelines: A Captivating Collection of Tiger Football Stories.* Champaign, IL: Sports Publishing L.L.C, 2002.

"For Gunter, 40th Season as Good as the First." *LSU Campus: LSU Highlights Spring 2004.* http://www.lsu.edu/highlights/041/gunter.html.

Hardesty, Dan. *The Louisiana Tigers: LSU Football.* Huntsville, AL: The Strode Publishers, 1975.

Helman, David. "Softball, Current, Former Tigers Excited About Stadium Advancements." *Daily Reveille.* 16 Feb. 2009. http://www.lsureveille.com/softball/current/former/tigers/excited/about/stadium/advancements.

Hendrickson, Brian. "LSU Fans Prove to Be Class Act in Regionals." *Wilmington Star-News.* 2 June 2003. reprinted in *The Advocate.* 22 June 2003. http://docs.newsbank.com/s/InfoWeb/aggdocs/NewsBank..

Hunter, Bruce and Joe Planas. *Fighting Tigers Basketball.* Chicago: Bonus Books, Inc. 1991.

Hyams, Jimmy. "Risher & Tigers Upset Alabama, 20-10. *Greatest Moments in LSU Football History.* Francis J. Fitzgerald, ed. Champaign, IL: Sports

Publishing L.L.C., 2002. 112-15.

Kirkpatrick, Curry. "Shack Attack." *Sports Illustrated*. 21 Jan. 1991. http://
    sportsillustrated.cnn.com/vault/article/magazine/MAG 1118770/index.htm.

Lawrence, Andrew. "And Mingo Was His Name." *Sports Illustrated*. 15 April 2013.
    http://sportsillustrated.cnn.com/vault/article/magazine/MAG1207388/
    index.htm.

Lowe, Kent, Sr. "Look Back: 20 Years after LSU, Loyola Marymount." *LSUsports.
    net*. 3 Feb. 2010. http://www.lsusports.net/ViewArticle.dbml.

"LSU Claims 5th NCAA Golf Title to End 60 Year Drought." *ESPN.go.com*. 3 June
    2015. http://espn.go.com/collegesports/story/_/id/1300672.

"LSU Football Traditions A to Z." *2009 LSU Football Media Guide*. 60-65. http://
    www.lsusports.net/ViewArticle.dbml.

McCartney, Cory. "A Tiger Unchained." *Sports Illustrated Presents LSU Tigers:
    2007 National Champions*. 16 Jan. 2008. 47-49

-----. "One Title Down, One More to Go." *Sports Illustrated Presents LSU Tigers:
    2007 National Champions*. 16 Jan. 2008. 35.

McMahon, Tim. "Brandon Bass' Camp Is Just the Beginning." *Dallas Mavericks
    Blog*. 21 June 2008, http://mavsblog.dallasnews.com/archives/2008/06.

Mule, Marty. *Game of My Life: LSU: Memorable Stories of Tigers Football*.
    Champaign, IL: Sports Publishing L.L.C., 2006.

-----. *Eye of the Tiger: A Hundred Years of LSU Football*. Atlanta: Longstreet
    Press, 1993.

Murphy, Austin. "The 2007 BCS Championship." *Sports Illustrated Presents LSU
    Tigers: 2007 National Champions*. 16 Jan. 2008. 36-44.

Rabalais, Scott. "LSU Stays Alive with High Drama." *The Advocate*. 21 May 2000.
    http://docs.newsbank.com/s/InfoWeb/aggdocs/NewsBank.

-----. "LSU's Robinson Enjoys Practice: Relishes Chance to Play Game He Almost
    Lost." *The Advocate*. 26 March 2002. http://docs.newsbank.com/s.Info
    Web/aggdocs/NewsBank.

Rosetta, Randy. "Big Makeover: A Slimmer and Trimmer Davis Motivated to
    Give Tigers Boost." *The Advocate*. 30 July 2006. http://docs.newsbank.
    com/s/InfoWeb/aggdocs/NewsBank.

-----. "Giving Back: Bass Helping Underprivileged at Camp." *The Advocate*. 18
    July 2008. http://docs.newsbank.com/s/InfoWeb/aggdocs/NewsBank.

"Shoot out the Moon: More to Pete Maravich Than the 'Pistol.'" *LSU Campus: LSU
    Highlights Spring 2005*. http://www.lsu.edu/highlights/051/maravich.html.

Stafford, Will. "NATIONAL CHAMPIONS! Men's Golf Beats USC, 4-1." *LSUsports.
    net*. 4 June 2015, http://www.lsusports.net/ViewArticle.dbml?

Tiger Terrific! LSU's Unforgettable 2003 Championship Season. Chicago:
    Triumph Books, 2004.

Warner, Chris, ed. *SEC Sports Quotes*. Baton Rouge: CEW Enterprises, 2002.

"Warren Morris." *TheGoal.com*. http://www.thegoal.com.players/baseball/
    warren_morris/morris21_warren.html.

West, Marvin. "In a Difficult Hour, The Torch Is Passed." *The Greatest Moments
    in LSU Football History*. Francis J. Fitzgerald, ed. Champaign, IL: Sports
    Publishing L.L.C., 2002. 106-111.

Wickes, Frank B. "LSU Band History." *LSU Department of Bands*. http://www.
    bands.lsu.edu/band_history/index.php.